"Fr. Charles Cummings's revised *Monastic Practices* is an insider's guide to life in the monastic world. Although specifically directed at monastics, it offers secular readers much worthy of pondering value. Drawing on his lifetime in a Trappist abbey, Fr. Charles offers a richly austere, very beautiful volume. For many topics, Fr. Charles provides both the historical practice and the ways in which it has been modified more recently, assisting someone living in community to understand some of the more mystifying customs, or a secular reader to comprehend something of the way monks adapt to the changing world. The meditative bits that appear scattered throughout—discussion of silence, the quality of the cell, and the presence of death—add to the overall balance between instruction and reflection, history and now, individual and community that make *Monastic Practices* a distinctive and valuable contribution to the body of monastic literature."

—Marjory Lange
Western Oregon University

Timothy Waid
Saint Vincent Archabbey
300 Fraser Purchase Rd
Latrobe, PA 15650

MONASTIC WISDOM SERIES: NUMBER FORTY-SEVEN

Monastic Practices

Charles Cummings, ocso

Revised Edition

α

Cistercian Publications
www.cistercianpublications.org

LITURGICAL PRESS
Collegeville, Minnesota
www.litpress.org

A Cistercian Publications title published by Liturgical Press

Cistercian Publications
Editorial Offices
161 Grosvenor Street
Athens, Ohio 54701
www.cistercianpublications.org

Illustrations by M. Bernarda Seferovich, OCist.

Unless otherwise indicated, excerpts from the documents of the Second Vatican Council are taken from the Vatican website.

Library of Congress Cataloging-in-Publication Data

Cummings, Charles, 1940–
    Monastic practices / by Charles Cummings, OCSO. — Second Edition.
        pages   cm. — (Monastic wisdom series ; number forty-seven)
    ISBN 978-0-87907-050-2 — ISBN 978-0-87907-484-5 (ebook)
    1. Monastic and religious life.   2. Spiritual life—Catholic Church.
  I. Title.

    BX2435.C83   2015
    248.8'94—dc23   2015024983

CONTENTS

these things that have been written
are written for our instruction

INTRODUCTION

The traditional practices of the monastic life are directly connected with our search for God. These practices—sacred reading, liturgical prayer, work, silence, asceticism, and many others—are concrete ways and means by which we in monasteries seek God. In and through these practices we express our spiritual values and daily live out our vowed commitment to God. Our monastic life in its outward practices as well as its inward spirit is totally oriented toward seeking and finding God.

Sometimes it may not be completely obvious, especially for newcomers to monastic life, that a particular practice such as rising long before dawn and keeping watch can foster and facilitate our journey toward God. Or, if the value of such a practice did seem clear to us at an earlier stage of our monastic life, it may no longer seem important now that we have reached greater maturity in our vocation. In either case, the practice loses its meaning for us and becomes merely another exercise to put up with, a lifeless formality to go through each day. The practice has lost its original power, and we get nothing out of it any more.

The question, as the Lord put it to the prophet Ezekiel, is "Son of man, can these bones come back to life?" (Ezek 37:3).[1]

The following chapters will explore common monastic practices in order to rediscover them as viable means of leading contemporary monks and nuns to a deeper encounter with God in faith, hope, and love. These traditional practices will be viable, in the sense of being at the service of life, if we know how to use them and how to give ourselves to them until they lead us to God. This is a "how to" book more than a theological or historical study of monastic customs. It is not only newcomers who need to appreciate the traditional monastic practices. The rest of us can discover still deeper levels of meaning, for example, in our interactions with others in the community or in the time we spend alone in our cell or in the common rituals we perform as we move through the monastic schedule. For monks and nuns, the ordinary things we do every day constitute the normal path to God. In the art of living the monastic life, we are always beginners, beginning anew our search for God, because there is always more of the triune, living God to be discovered.

External monastic practices are one thing—their inner spirit is another. The structural framework of observances exists to give support and form to the vivifying spirit of love. That spirit is in the way we do what we do and in our motivation for doing it. In focusing on external monastic practices, we run the danger of a kind of rubricism, as if following the rubrics of monastic living could magically unite us to God. What does unite each of us to God is the living faith, hope, and love that animate our heart and behavior. Monastic practices express those interior attitudes but cannot substitute for them. When the external practices are in harmony with interior attitudes of faith and love, our daily life is transformed, and the kingdom of God becomes a reality in our midst.

Reflections on the meaning and implementation of monastic practices are always provisional, always open to further insights. Although my own monastic experience is limited to the Trappist-Cistercian tradition, I have tried to situate these practices

---

[1] Unless otherwise indicated, Scripture translations are from the *New American Bible, Revised Edition*.

in the common Western monastic tradition of Saint Benedict, the Desert Fathers and Mothers, and the Bible, with some references to other traditions as well.

My reflections are made with a view to both monks and nuns, for all the practices are common to monasteries of women and men. In fact, some of these practices are common to all forms of consecrated life and receive special emphasis even in non-monastic communities. A selective, prudent use of these practices also might benefit persons outside the monastery who wish to follow traditional Christian methods of spiritual deepening.

This revised edition of *Monastic Practices* updates, corrects, and slightly expands the first edition. I wish to thank very much the many editors and advisors, almost too many to mention by name, who have helped me in this task. I especially want to thank Sr. M. Bernarda Seferovich, OCist., for her thoughtful and clever drawings, which have joyfully introduced and illuminated each chapter of both editions of this book. Appreciative responses from readers of the first edition prompted me to improve the book as best I can, without detriment to its original purpose. Finally, it should be noted that opinions expressed here are the personal interpretations of the author and not the authorized statements of any monastic family.

man does not live on bread alone

but by every word that comes from the mouth of god

SACRED READING

The monastic style of life that evolved in the West after the Desert Fathers and Saint Benedict stands on three foundation stones. Liturgical prayer, manual work, and sacred reading, that is, *lectio divina*, constitute the threefold footing of our daily monastic life. Jesus Christ himself is the ultimate foundation stone, and these three practices connect us to him. The personal stability of each monk or nun in the monastic vocation depends in part on this triadic foundation. If we attempt to build the whole structure of our monastic life on just one foot of the tripod, or even on two, it may all come crashing down some stormy day. A triple footing provides a foundation that is firm against storms and trials.

The numerous other practices of monastic life cluster around liturgical prayer, work, and sacred reading like stringers and trusses that tie a structure together and make it an integral whole. Our study of monastic practices begins with a consideration of each of the three principal supports, starting with sacred reading, because it may be the most problematic. Afterward, we will go on to liturgical prayer and then to monastic work.

1

Sacred Reading as Encounter

Although there are special challenges to be faced in our postliterate age, we all have the capability and the grace to become masters in the art of sacred reading. Reading has lost its savor for many in our culture and has been replaced by audiovisual media of communication. At the same time, the volume of printed material has soared. There is too much information to absorb. The result is a tension between contemporary habits and the slow, reflective reading typical of traditional sacred reading.

Historically, reading has been a major component of the monastic day. Saint Benedict allotted two or three hours a day to sacred reading in summer and up to five hours during the winter. His principle was to allow as much time as possible for sacred reading after the daily manual labor was completed: "Idleness is the enemy of the soul. Therefore the brothers should have specified periods for manual labor as well as for prayerful reading [*lectio divina*]" (RB 48.1).[1]

The high value monks have placed on sacred reading comes from the conviction that in this practice we meet God through the instrumentality of the inspired text. Before the fifteenth century there were no periods set aside in the monastic schedule for meditative prayer. The common way of communing with God was sacred reading; this was the monastic method of meditation. The monk or nun would sit with the text of Scripture and begin to read attentively and reflectively until a word or phrase or scene struck the imagination or the heart. At that moment the reader

---

[1] Translations of excerpts from the Rule of Saint Benedict are taken from *The Rule of Saint Benedict 1980*, ed. Timothy Fry (Collegeville, MN: Liturgical Press, 1981). The term *lectio divina* apparently was first used by Origen in a letter to Gregory the Miracle-Worker (see Sources Chrétiennes 148: 192). The term *spiritual reading* originated with the Jesuits in the sixteenth or seventeenth century as an approximate translation of *lectio divina* (see *Dictionnaire de Spiritualité* 9: 500). *Sacred reading*, as used in this chapter, is an attempt at a more adequate translation of *lectio divina*. The medieval history of *lectio divina* is competently investigated by Duncan Robertson, *Lectio Divina: The Medieval Experience of Reading*, CS 238 (Collegeville, MN: Cistercian Publications, 2011). Cistercian author Michael Casey presents the art of *lectio divina* with a view to helping those who live outside monasteries in his book *Sacred Reading: The Ancient Art of* Lectio Divina (Liguori, MO: Liguori/Triumph, 1996).

paused, put the text aside, and gave himself or herself to prayer. The prayerful pause might last less than a minute or might be extended for a number of minutes. When attention faltered, the reader would return to the text until another moment of insight or another incentive to love should come along. The rhythm of reading and pausing would continue peacefully, unhurriedly, until the bell announced the next exercise of the monastic day.[2]

Listening and Responding

Sacred reading allows the Word of God to touch and awaken the heart. "Indeed," says the Letter to the Hebrews, "the word of God is living and effective, sharper than any two-edged sword . . . able to discern reflections and thoughts of the heart" (Heb 4:12). When we spend time in sacred reading, we invite God's Word to penetrate our heart and to evoke from that deepest center of our being a response of surrender, wonder, praise, regret, petition, love.

In the words that we read, God speaks to us; in our prayerful pauses we respond to God, verbally or wordlessly. Sacred reading has this double articulation of listening to the Word and responding to the Word. Continual reading, without the periodic pauses, may be a pious exercise and even an appropriate way of praying at times when we are exhausted or distracted, but it is not sacred reading, strictly speaking. The true dynamic of sacred reading is captured in the following description, by the poet and novelist Rainer Maria Rilke, of a man reading: "He does not always remain bent over his pages; he often leans back and closes his eyes over a line he has been reading again, and its meaning spreads through his blood."[3]

---

[2] Sacred reading was a holistic activity that integrated imagination, memory, affections, will, and even speech and hearing. It was customary until the late Middle Ages to pronounce the words in a low tone. The effect was to inscribe the sacred text physiologically in the reader's mind and memory, resulting in a phenomenal recall of terms and themes from various parts of Scripture that shed light on one another. See Jean Leclercq, *Love of Learning and Desire for God* (New York: Mentor-Omega, 1962), 78–79.

[3] Rainer Maria Rilke, *The Notebooks of Malte Laurids Brigge*, trans. M. D. Herter Norton (New York: W. W. Norton, 1949), 201.

Sacred reading is a process of assimilating the word of God and letting its meaning spread through our blood into every part of our being, a process of impregnation, interiorization, personalization of the word of God. Yet the process is a gentle one. The Lord does not come in an earthquake but in a soft, whispering sound (1 Kgs 19:22). In the course of our sacred reading, we meet the Lord in living faith, hope, and love. The encounter takes place without drama as we quietly savor and relish the mystery of God's caring presence. The encounter is real without being extraordinary or spectacular.[4]

As with any method of prayer, the effects of sacred reading should become evident over a long period of time in a person's life. Repeated encounters with the word of God will bring about a gradual transformation as our thinking and willing become progressively harmonized with God's will. Slowly we grow in interior freedom and lose our innate orientation toward comfort and security. Our monastic predecessors in past centuries lived by God's word in Scripture, thought in its categories, spoke in its language, and wrote as if they had a biblical concordance connected to their pen. These were fruits of a lifetime of sacred reading. Speaking at a large gathering of Scripture scholars in 2005, Pope Benedict XVI said, "If this practice is promoted with efficacy, I am convinced that it will produce a new spiritual springtime in the Church."[5]

Obstacles to Sacred Reading

Circumstances may prevent the experience of sacred reading from being fruitful. The text may be inappropriate to one's current ability because of its difficulty or to one's current needs because

---

[4] Sacred reading can, of course, be the occasion for God to act quite powerfully through a word that seems aimed directly at the reader. For an example, see Marylee Mitcham, *An Accidental Monk* (Cincinnati, OH: St. Anthony Messenger Press, 1976), 35.

[5] "Benedict XVI Promotes Biblical Meditation," *Zenit*, September 16, 2005, Code ZE05091608, http://www.zenit.org/english/visualizza .phtml?sid=76678/.

of its content. Not all the books of the Bible are equally inspiring, though all are the inspired word of God. When nonbiblical material is selected for sacred reading, the author's style of writing or the limitations of his or her cultural background or scientific inaccuracies may be major distractions. The writings of some of the saints contain timeless truths about the spiritual life, but these are hidden like nuggets of gold amid piles of base material. At some point the reader has to make an honest decision about whether a particular text is worth staying with for sacred reading. Part of the art of sacred reading is selecting the appropriate text.

On the reader's part, a common obstacle to sacred reading is impatience. If we expect to receive lofty insights from every line of the text, our expectations are doomed to disappointment. Impatience drives us to another book. The reader who trusts in the power of the text to communicate God's living word, however, will be prepared to give the text adequate time, to dwell with the text, to engage it with a feeling for its mystery. God can communicate his word of life on many levels of meaning. Sometimes a patient openness to levels beyond the literal is needed in order to tap the life-giving springs. More will be said later about these levels of meaning.

Impatience also manifests itself in a voracious appetite to read more and more books and never to go back over a book a second time. We may have a long list of spiritual books we want to get through or a reading program that will take us through the entire Bible in six months. The compulsive urge to finish this book and get on to the next one prevents us from pausing to pray. Without the rhythmic alternation between listening and responding, sacred reading becomes reading for information or edification. True sacred reading is slowed-down reading and rereading with no regrets for the time thus spent. As Scripture scholar Francis Martin pointed out, "Prayerful reading happens in an atmosphere of 'wasting time.' There are no practical goals, no book to get through, no certain number of pages to read, but simply a deep sacramental use of God's word as a meeting place for God and man."[6]

---

[6] Francis Martin, "Prayerful Reading," *New Covenant* 2 (July 1972): 14.

Speed reading or scanning a text is useful and even necessary for digesting the contents of textbooks, periodicals, or newspapers. When the time for sacred reading comes, however, we have to be able to read slowly and patiently, in a relaxed and open spirit, ready to "taste and see that the Lord is good" (Ps 34:9). A businessman, Sidney Piddington, tells how he discovered the "special joys of super-slow reading" during three years of confinement in a Japanese prisoner-of-war camp in Singapore. Trying to make his precious book last as long as possible, he disciplined himself to linger over each page and enter into the experience being described by the author. His reading fell naturally into the rhythm of listening and responding. As he describes it, "Sometimes just a particular phrase caught my attention, sometimes a sentence. I would read it slowly, analyze it, read it again—perhaps changing down into an even lower gear—and then sit for twenty minutes thinking about it before moving on."[7]

Not only did slowing down make the book last longer, but as a bonus Piddington discovered that the practice lifted him above the sordidness and senselessness of prison-camp life and put him into a more humane world. Super-slow reading preserved his sanity, his human dignity, and his inner freedom. If we transpose this experience to a faith context, we can see that a slowed-down style of reading can be a key that opens the door through which God manifests himself to those who search for him. A hasty impatience prevents us from entering this world of revealed mystery.

Another obstacle to sacred reading is today's lack of a biblical consciousness. Our culture has lost much of its familiarity with biblical stories, biblical symbols, biblical persons, places, and ritual practices. Authors and preachers can no longer make biblical allusions and be sure that the majority of the audience will understand the reference. Why have we lost this familiarity with the Bible? Possibly because the Bible has been crowded out of our consciousness by a multitude of other books and media that compete for our limited attention span. Living in the age

[7] Sidney Piddington, "The Special Joys of Super-Slow Reading," *Reader's Digest* 52 (June 1973): 158.

of information and instant communication means that we are overloaded with information. Today the Bible, the word of God, is just one source of information competing with all the others.[8]

Immediate Preparation

When I have selected an appropriate text and resolved to spend time in patient, prayerful reading, what is the next step? Experience suggests that sacred reading is easier when I do it at a particular time and a particular place each day, and when I invoke the assistance of the Holy Spirit. Learning the art of sacred reading is at first a methodical and systematic process; more is involved than merely opening a book and sitting down to read.

Time. Sacred reading can be prolonged, but perhaps twenty minutes would be the minimum time to set apart for this exercise. A certain amplitude of time seems needed for the listening and responding to become a rhythmic process. Experimentation will help us discover our best time of day for sacred reading. Perhaps the early morning, before the bustle of the day's activity has begun; or perhaps the evening hour when work is over and we are ready to quiet down. Ideally we should do sacred reading at a time when we are alert and will not have to spend all our energy fighting off sleep. Perhaps a cup of coffee, or some physical exercises, or two minutes of total relaxation might leave us feeling sufficiently awake for serious sacred reading.

Place. A suitable place for sacred reading is a place readily available where we feel at home and will not be disturbed. We may have more than one favorite place for sacred reading—our cell, or a corner of the library, or a certain tree in the courtyard. Physical solitude is not absolutely necessary for sacred reading, though such privacy would permit us to read aloud without disturbing others. Nor is it necessary to seek the presence of the

---

[8] For a more extensive treatment of the obstacles to sacred reading, see Susan Muto, *A Practical Guide to Spiritual Reading* (Denville, NJ: Dimension Books, 1976), chap. 2. Writing out the text and writing one's response are also means of slowing down the reading. Muto suggests keeping a spiritual-reading notebook.

Blessed Sacrament for sacred reading. God is everywhere, but we will meet God primarily in the text when we do sacred reading. We may wish to reserve the church for a different form of prayer, one more wordless and contemplative or one more liturgical and communal. Saint Benedict wrote: "The oratory ought to be what it is called, and nothing else be done or stored there" (RB 52.1). Still, if we find that the church facilitates our sacred reading, then that should be the place for us. We will do sacred reading wherever we can be ourselves and be at peace.

Being at Peace. The listening involved in sacred reading presupposes a level of relaxed peacefulness and quiet receptivity on the reader's part. If our feelings and emotions are in turmoil, how can we hear the word of God? If we are full of tension and preoccupations, these will soon surface when we attempt to read. We need to create an inner space for the word, a space free of all worries, a free space. How do we calm down before reading? Our whole monastic life should be slowly calming us, freeing us from cares, creating in us that purity of heart that is the ideal soil for the word of God to take root and grow. If we are feeling restless at the beginning of sacred reading, a few deep breaths of fresh air may help to gather our forces and center our attention on the matter at hand. A prayer may serve to make our desires explicit.

Supplication. Sacred reading is a grace-guided activity. There was wisdom in the pious custom that formerly directed the monastic reader to kneel for a moment to pray for the Spirit's assistance before beginning sacred reading and even to kneel while reading the first few words of the biblical text. Fruitful sacred reading is not simply the result of our own efforts but also the work of grace. A brief prayer for God's help (almost any verse of Psalm 119 [118] is appropriate) expresses our faith in his power to enter our life and speak personally to us through the text in our hands. Prayer also disposes us to recognize the moment in our reading when we should pause and make our response to God's word.[9]

---

[9] On the immediate preparation for sacred reading see also Felix Donahue, "*Lectio* in Our Life," *Monastic Exchange* 8, no. 2 (Summer 1976): 63–65; and Louis Bouyer, *Introduction to Spirituality* (New York: Desclée, 1961), 53–55.

The Ladder of Guigo

From a twelfth-century Carthusian prior named Guigo II we have a letter with a detailed description of the monastic method of sacred reading.[10] Guigo distinguished four stages or rungs: reading, meditation, prayer, contemplation. "These," he said, "make a ladder for monks by which they rise from earth to heaven." Guigo's ladder still has value for us today, provided we understand that it bears the defects of all schematizations of the spiritual life. Our own personal ladder may have more rungs than Guigo's, or we may sometimes skip a rung or two under the inspiration of the Holy Spirit. There are also individuals who have problems with any structured form of prayer and prefer jumping into the Bible at random.

Reading and meditation, the first two rungs on the ladder, are climbed by our grace-assisted natural powers. At the third rung, prayer, we are partly active, partly acted on by God. On the highest rung (contemplation), the word of God lifts and draws us, carrying us into itself. The four rungs of Guigo's ladder amplify what I have been calling the prayerful rhythm of listening and then responding. Reading is listening to God's word, while meditation, prayer, and contemplation are degrees of responding to God's word. The four rungs are not four steps in a recipe that has to be followed carefully each time; they are a description of what usually happens when the reader contacts the word of God and lets it reverberate throughout the different levels of his or her inner being, beginning with the outermost level and moving progressively deeper.

Rhythm of Prayer

It will be helpful to explore briefly the dynamics of each of the four rungs of the ladder of reading proposed by Guigo. He tells

---

[10] Guigo II, *The Ladder of Monks and Twelve Meditations*, trans. Edmund Colledge and James Walsh (Garden City, NY: Image Books, 1978); also CS 48 (Kalamazoo, MI: Cistercian Publications, 1981). The next quotation in the paragraph is from the Image Books edition, p. 82, slightly altered.

us first that *reading* is a careful and attentive survey of the text in order to grasp the central idea. We begin to listen to the text by reading it slowly and attentively. Vocalizing slows the pace and helps imprint words on the memory. What is being said? What is the meaning of this episode or of this phrase? What is the truth being communicated? We are interpreting the words before us, trying to uncover everything they conceal. Perhaps a single word captures our attention. If we wish, we may concentrate on this word, murmur it aloud, even sing it if we can pick out its inmost rhythm. We listen more and more to the text until we understand it as fully as we can.

The next stage is to ponder the text in *meditation*, examining it in relation to other similar texts, turning it over in our mind, asking questions, noticing even what is not said. Reasoning is the primary tool used in meditation as we probe for the underlying meaning. There is also an affective and personal note as we permit ourselves to hear the words as if they were spoken to us, as a message for us. Meditation is the Marian stage of treasuring the word and pondering it in our heart (Luke 2:19, 31). We believe that God is speaking to us personally through this text, and we take his word to heart. By reflecting and mulling over God's word, we assimilate it and let it become a living part of us. As this truth touches our inmost self, it is no longer we who are interpreting it; now we are letting it interpret us and show us to ourselves as if in a mirror. The light of spiritual truth illumines weaknesses in us that we have not wished to face. The word of God is a judgment on our infidelities and disposes us to pray for grace, mercy, and the fulfillment of our spiritual longings.

In the stage of *prayer* our awareness shifts from the text to the divine author, from the written word to the unwritten Word of God. We dialogue with this Word in the interiority of our heart, in direct, personal conversation, with completely uncensored and spontaneous freedom, with the urgency of a beggar asking for a crumb of bread or a drop of water. We pour out to God our feelings and desires, even asking to know him face to face if his mercy permits. We surrender to his will communicated through the text. As we respond to various texts, gratitude may predominate, or repentance even with tears, or intercession and petition, or loving adoration. Without feeling hurried or rushed, we spend time with the Lord who knows all that we need before we ask for it (see Matt 6:32). Under the impulse of grace our affective prayer may pass into the fourth stage.

In the state of *contemplation*, we desire simply to rest in God and remain with God. We know that God is near. We experience God's nearness as a gentle, caring presence, the presence of a loving father or mother. From this benevolent source we are ready to receive all that we need to live on. There is no need now for words or thoughts. Our words and thoughts are absorbed into this loving awareness of a silent presence. We meet the Lord in the mysterious silence created around us and within us. On a deep interior level we sense a soothing calm, a refreshment for our weariness, satisfaction for our yearning, anointing with "the oil of gladness" (Ps 45:7). Then, before we are fully aware of who or what is present, the spell is broken by a passing distraction. Our restless imagination has interrupted the fragile encounter.

When distractions put an end to restful communing with God, we have several options. We can thank God for his gracious mercy and then terminate our period of sacred reading. If we wish to continue sacred reading, we can return to the stage of meditation or prayer or take up the book again and read the next passage. "Like the angels ascending and descending Jacob's ladder, [our] attention [can] go up and down the steps of the ladder of consciousness."[11] In fact, nothing prevents us from going back to the text we read originally in order to re-read it. Because we have already gone through it, this text will reverberate with special meaning, as if we were running our hand over the strings of a harp and resonating with each separate note on different levels within us. Sacred reading entails re-reading.

As a rhythm of prayer, sacred reading means listening, then responding, then resting, then going back to listen again either to a new text or to the same text with fresh docility. Each time we

---

[11] Thomas Keating, "Contemplative Prayer in the Christian Tradition," *America* 138 (April 8, 1978): 279.

approach the text in a loving, listening way, it can yield a new layer of meaning, like peeling off layer after layer of something that never diminishes in size. The Holy Spirit assists in this activity, disclosing truths, setting the heart afire, and leading the reader into the Sabbath rest of contemplation (see Luke 24:32 and Heb 4:9-10).

Fruits of Sacred Reading

Continual exposure to the power of the word of God in sacred reading will have noticeable effects on the reader. Gradually, with divine grace, the word will become flesh in the reader's daily life. He or she will become not merely a hearer, but a doer, of the word (Luke 6:47). Sacred reading makes an opening through which the life-giving word of God can enter the reader's heart and carry on its work of healing and transforming. The word, once received, is received more readily the next time.

The habit of listening during sacred reading fosters the attitude of listening in other situations to what the word of God is asking. The habit of mulling over words and phrases or murmuring them aloud promotes the practice of repeating short, spontaneous prayers during free moments or while working. Fidelity to sacred reading should produce a gradual change in the reader's relationships with other people, helping him or her become more generous, considerate, gentle, and less selfish, cranky, gossipy, touchy. Sacred reading spreads out into daily life as a power of ongoing reformation and conversion, enabling the reader to recognize and respond to the word of God spoken at diverse times and circumstances. Liturgical prayer, for instance, is a privileged place of encounter with the word of God. Sacred reading and liturgical prayer complement each other and are not intended to remain separate activities competing for a person's time. The psalms, hymns, and readings of the Divine Office come to life as they furnish occasions for brief but intense experiences of meditation, prayer, and contemplation.[12]

---

[12] One monk has described his experience during Vespers as follows: "After the choral psalmody, the monks sat down and the reader took up his

Extension of Sacred Reading

I have been discussing sacred reading as if Scripture were the only text that could lead to "the supreme good of knowing Christ Jesus my Lord" (Phil 3:8). Scripture is the preferred material for monastic sacred reading, but God speaks in many ways. The concept of sacred reading is flexible enough to extend far beyond the books of the Bible. When one has mastered the art of sacred reading by learning how to perceive God speaking in Scripture, one possesses a tool that may be used fruitfully with nonscriptural material. Ultimately, it is not what we read but how we read it that is important; if we know how to read something in such a way that it nourishes our heart and rouses our spirit to pray, then it counts as sacred reading.

After Scripture, the writings of the saints are perhaps the most rewarding texts to explore in sacred reading. Works of spiritual masters both living and dead, biographies of the saints, devotional literature, and poetry can be used for sacred reading.[13] Other literature, such as T. S. Eliot's *Murder in the Cathedral*, Helen Keller's *The Story of My Life*, and C. S. Lewis's *The Chronicles of Narnia*, which cannot be classified as devotional, may, nevertheless, be sensitive to the deeper mysteries of life and draw attention to ultimate values. These classic and contemporary writings can sometimes speak forcefully to the reader and become a place where God's word is encountered.

---

book and began the scheduled reading for the 'Saturday of the Fifth Week of Easter,' taken from one of St. Augustine's discourses on the Psalms. . . . 'What we commemorate before Easter is what we experience in this life; what we celebrate after Easter points to something we do not yet possess. This is why we keep the first season with fasting and prayer; *but now the fast is over.*' That is as much as I heard. At the words 'now the fast is over' by spontaneous association the words from the Song of Songs sprang from my memory, 'and the winter is over and gone, come my beloved, come!' A prayer of desire and gratitude flamed out and filled the minutes of silence after the reader sat down" (A Monk of New Clairvaux, *Don't You Belong to Me?* [New York: Paulist Press, 1979], 139–40. See all of chap. 10, "The Way of *Lectio Divina*").

[13] For illustrations of these and other categories, see Muto, *A Practical Guide*, 4–17.

Once the practice is learned, sacred reading can be extended beyond written words to *auditio divina*, inspirational music, to *visio divina*, contemplating sacred art or a sunset or kittens at play, and extended even to *video divina*, watching an inspirational video. God speaks his word even in nonverbal language. God speaks eloquently in the great book of nature. Saint Bernard, who was surely a lover of the written word, also loved to walk in the forests and fields, sensing the vastness of God's presence.[14] Many monasteries are located in places of great scenic beauty that invites a contemplative response.

Even human-made objects of beauty may be the book, so to speak, where one reads of God. In the Middle Ages, the illiterate could understand the message of illuminated manuscripts, sculpted capitals on the pillars of the church or cloister, and stained-glass windows, which were called "the Bible of the poor."[15] God also speaks in the events of each person's daily life and in the larger events that affect the course of human history. Someone skilled in sacred reading can look back at the course of his or her own life and read there the record of God's wise and loving activity. As Matthias Neuman has written, "Here unfolds the deepest meaning of *lectio* as a reading, the reading of one's own life-history as ongoing dialogue of grace and conversion of life toward the Mystery of God."[16]

At the beginning of his third sermon on the Song of Songs, Saint Bernard wrote, "Today the text we are to study is the book

[14] Writing to Henry Murdac, Saint Bernard said, "Believe me who have experience, you will find much more laboring among the woods than you ever will amongst books. Woods and stones will teach you what you can never hear from any master" (*The Letters of St. Bernard of Clairvaux*, trans. Bruno Scott James; London: Burns Oates, 1953 [Letter 106] 107, p. 156. See also William of St. Thierry, *Sancti Bernardi Vita* 5.26; and St. Bernard, *Apologia* 12.30, CF 1 [Kalamazoo, MI: Cistercian Publications], 68).

[15] Apart from the subject matter of the stained glass windows, the beauty of their bright ruby-and-blue colors was in itself inspiring even to such cultured people as Abbot Suger of Saint-Denis. See his remarks quoted in *New Catholic Encyclopedia*, 1967 ed., s.v. "Stained Glass," 631.

[16] Matthias Neuman, "The Contemporary Spirituality of the Monastic *Lectio*," *Review for Religious* 36 (January 1977): 110. See his entire discussion of material for sacred reading.

of our own experience."[17] When we have learned to read God's word in the book of our everyday life, then we are aware of a continuity integrating all that we do in the course of the day. Everything promises a potential encounter with the Word—not only sacred reading, but work and liturgical prayer, interaction with others, appreciation of nature, music, art—everything may become a medium through which the Word speaks to us.

When everything is sacred reading, however, the practice may become diluted to the point of vanishing. In order for our whole monastic life to be an encounter with the person of Christ, specific times must be set aside for encountering him through sacred reading in the strict sense. Only when "the words of God ring in the ear of his heart," as Saint Gregory the Great says, can the reader hear that voice resounding everywhere he or she turns.[18] Sacred reading can be extended to embrace the whole of monastic life provided it is also maintained as a distinct monastic practice. As Sr. Margaret Mary Hanron observes, "It could be said that *lectio divina*, in its broadest connotation, is coextensive with the entire life of the monk. In this understanding, *lectio* in its usual sense would be the form, the pattern, the place, and even the 'sacrament' of that broader *lectio* which is an ineffable and uninterrupted communion of prayer, increasingly pervading the whole existence of the monk."[19]

Concluding Examples

The actual experience of sacred reading is something quite simple. There is the text, there is the reader, and there is the Spirit of God. When these elements come together, almost anything

---

[17] Bernard of Clairvaux, *On the Song of Songs I*, trans. Kilian Walsh, CF 4 (Spencer, MA: Cistercian Publications, 1971), 16.

[18] Gregory the Great, *Homiliae in Evangelia* 1, hom. 18.1, *Sanctorum Patrum Opuscula Selecta*, ed. H. Hurter (Oeniponte [Innsbruck]: Libraria Academica Wagneriana, 1892), 118, http://books.google.com/books/reader?id=8OFAyNEfPbsC&printsec=frontcover&output=reader&pg=GBS.PA118.

[19] Margaret Mary Hanron, "Lectio Divina and Study in St. Bernard and at Present," *Hallel* 1 (November 1974): 23, also 31. See also Ivan Illich, *In the Vineyard of the Text: A Commentary to Hugh's Didascalicon* (Chicago and London: University of Chicago Press, 1993), 58–61.

may happen. The reader needs to proceed with spontaneity and playfulness. Everyone has the right to approach sacred reading in his or her own creative and highly personal way without feeling obliged to imitate such medieval models as Guigo the Carthusian or even to keep in mind all the matters discussed in the present chapter. In this discussion, a fundamentally simple reality has been subjected to an analysis that might make sacred reading seem intimidating, especially to beginners. This chapter will therefore now conclude with two illustrations of sacred reading that may serve to bring the foregoing discussion down to earth.

The examples will be from Scripture, one from each Testament. Our text from the Old Testament is Psalm 23, and from the New Testament it is Luke 21:5-10. An unhurried, attentive reading of the whole passage is followed by a prayerful reflection and response. Paragraph divisions indicate the successive steps of Guigo's ladder. The moments of wordless communing cannot be captured in print, though these contemplative pauses are the soul of sacred reading. The following, then, are not so much models to be imitated as concrete examples, portrayed in print, of one reader encountering a sacred text in the presence of the Spirit of God.

Example 1. I begin with a short prayer: "Come, Holy Spirit, fill the heart of your servant and open for me your life-giving Word."

Text of Psalm 23

>The Lord is my shepherd;
>there is nothing I lack.
>In green pastures he makes me lie down;
>to still waters he leads me; he restores my soul.
>He guides me along right paths
>for the sake of his name.
>Even though I walk through the valley of the shadow of death,
>I will fear no evil, for you are with me;
>your rod and your staff comfort me.
>You set a table before me in front of my enemies;
>You anoint my head with oil; my cup overflows.
>Indeed, goodness and mercy will pursue me

all the days of my life;
I will dwell in the house of the LORD for endless days.

(*Reflection*) I notice that the figure of God as shepherd evolves toward the end of the psalm into a picture of God as the host of guests at a banquet. The image of the Lord as my shepherd is the one that speaks more to me right now. I recall other places where the theme of shepherd turns up, such as Ezekiel, "the lost I will search out, the strays I will bring back, the injured I will bind up, and the sick I will heal" (Ezek 34:16), or in John's gospel, "I am the good shepherd. A good shepherd lays down his life for the sheep" (John 10:11).

The Lord is the shepherd of Israel, the good shepherd who does not, like a hireling, abandon his sheep. He leads them to fresh, green pastures on the mountain slope. I get a visual image of an Alpine landscape with snow on the mountain peaks, a placid lake in the valley, and a large herd of sheep pasturing peacefully on the grassy slope. They lack nothing because they have a shepherd who loves and cares for each of them. I believe that I, too, am cared for like that. "There is nothing I lack." Even when I lose my way and wander into the dark valley of suffering and death, I have nothing to fear. My good shepherd will seek me out when I am lost and will bring me back on his own shoulders.

(*Prayer*) Lord, you are my good shepherd. You are there "with your rod and your staff." You are there with your cross as your rod and staff, that cross by which you won the right to be my shepherd and give me comfort in all my distress. Jesus, good shepherd, let me recognize your voice when you call me by name. Give me a place of repose, lead me into your rest. Make me trust more and more in your care for me. You have been a trustworthy shepherd thus far in my life. You led me to the fresh, green pastures of this place, and I want only to dwell here forever. When I injure myself, bind up my wound. When I fall sick, make me well again. When I am silly and stray off, guide me along the right path.

I feel myself being shepherded by your unseen hand, I feel that you are close to me. I want you to be my shepherd forever.

I surrender all my cares to your care for me. My Lord, my shepherd . . .

(I conclude with the Lord's Prayer.)

Example 2. I begin with a short prayer: "Come, Holy Spirit, fill the heart of your servant and open for me your life-giving Word."

Text of Luke 21:5-10:

> While some people were speaking about how the temple was adorned with costly stones and votive offerings, he said, "All that you see here—the days will come when there will not be left a stone upon another stone that will not be thrown down."
> Then they asked him, "Teacher, when will this happen? And what sign will there be when all these things are about to happen?" He answered, "See that you not be deceived, for many will come in my name, saying, 'I am he,' and 'The time has come.' Do not follow them! When you hear of wars and insurrections, do not be terrified; for such things must happen first, but it will not immediately be the end."

(*Reflection*) The Galilean disciples of Jesus were awestruck by the stonework of Herod's temple in Jerusalem, the immense blocks of perfectly fitting, gleaming white marble, the walls adorned with decorative ornaments donated for the honor of God. A huge grapevine of solid gold adorned the outside wall of the temple.

Jesus predicts that it will all come tumbling down. This did happen in AD 70, when the city fell to the Romans under Titus, and they burned the temple to rubble. Is Jesus telling me that every human construct is liable to come tumbling down, whether it be the tower of Babel, the commercial temple of the World Trade Center, the precarious temple of the stock exchange, or even the temple that is the monastery where I live, which is always vulnerable to fire or natural disaster? Or is Jesus talking about my personal temple that I have spent my life constructing—my career, my family, my reputation, my preferred path to God? Could it all come tumbling down? Like the crowd, I want to know "what sign will there be when all these things are about to happen?" Jesus gives several signs. "Many," he says, "will come in my name." They are here already; they sometimes stand on street corners carrying signs that say, "Warning! God's judgment is near." Jesus says, "Do not follow them!"

(Prayer) Lord Jesus, I ask your forgiveness for times when I have run after false messiahs, putting my trust in something or someone—even my own wisdom and strength—that is not you. Forgive me the times that I have followed after my passions—my greed, my gluttony, my lust, my anger, my pride—thinking that I had found the way to happiness, forgetting that you are the only way, truth, and life. Lord Jesus, I choose you now as my only Savior, my deepest love. I want to follow you alone, so that I will be secure when all the temples of this world tumble down around me. Let me never lose sight of you, Lord Jesus.

I believe that you are with me always and within me, protecting me and caring for me. I wish only to dwell in your loving presence, loving you in return all the days of my life. You are my temple. You are the only temple that will never come crashing down . . . .

(I conclude with the Lord's Prayer.)

Questions for Reflection

Why should you follow a structure for your sacred reading, such as the four rungs of Guigo's ladder?

What is your greatest obstacle to sacred reading, and how can you overcome this obstacle?

from sunrise to sunset my name is praised among the nations

and a clean oblation is offered everywhere to my name

LITURGICAL PRAYER

In liturgical prayer, as in sacred reading, we encounter the word of God, and our concern is to go from the sung or spoken word of God to a living encounter with the Word that is God. The words we meet in the liturgy are signs; the reality is the Word who cannot be expressed adequately in these signs but who can be discovered, praised, and loved in a personal relationship. The liturgy is a privileged means of fostering that personal relationship.

To explore the world of the liturgy in such a way as to draw from it its maximum spiritual benefit is a lifelong project. The power of the liturgy to transform and to lead us to God depends on our ability to immerse ourselves by grace in the mystery of Christ that is the objective content of the liturgy. We participate in liturgical prayer with our eye not so much on our artistic performance, our feelings, or our role in the ceremonies, but on God. As we worship and glorify God we are being transformed and sanctified through our unselfconscious involvement in the liturgical ritual.

Some degree of participation in community liturgical prayer is part of our life from the day we first come to the monastery. Year after year the liturgy leads us through the cycle of Christ's life. In this chapter we shall stop, look, and listen to what we are doing in liturgical prayer, so that the liturgy may help us go more deeply into the mystery of Christ's life and the meaning of our life in Christ.

After considering the place of liturgical prayer in monastic communities, we will sharpen our understanding of the signs that meet our bodily senses in the liturgy. With these considerations as background, we will discuss the structure of the Divine Office and the Eucharist. It will become clear that liturgical spirituality orients us toward the Paschal Mystery—the life, death, resurrection, and ascension of Jesus—as the model of our own deepest spiritual transformation.

Liturgy and Living

Liturgical prayer, primarily the Mass and Divine Office, should be seen in continuity with all our daily activities, not as something separate from the rest of our day or as a sacred moment stolen from ordinary activities and unconnected with the practical business of living. As we come together to pray, we bring with us the concerns we carry throughout the day and lay them before the Lord of blessing. Liturgical prayer is a center around which our other preoccupations are grouped like concentric rings, so that they are all influenced and blessed by that central core-activity where we encounter the living Christ, to whom nothing whatever is to be preferred (RB 72.11).[1]

---

[1] See *The Rule of Saint Benedict 1980*, ed. Timothy Fry (Collegeville, MN: Liturgical Press, 1981), 295. The mystery of Christ in his ongoing salvific and sanctifying activity is realized in the liturgy of Eucharist and Office. Simply to live in the "school for the Lord's service" (RB Prol. 45) has liturgical overtones if we think of the Greek root of *liturgy*, meaning "communal service." A text from the Second Vatican Council spells out the implication: "The principal duty of monks is to offer a service to the divine majesty at once humble and noble within the walls of the monastery, whether they dedicate themselves

Monasteries have fostered a tradition of excellence in the practice of liturgical prayer. To the liturgy we bring the best we have in musical and poetic talent, ceremonial vestments, buildings, and furnishings. We do this for the glory of God and not to become leaders in liturgical renewal, though monasteries have sometimes provided models for contemporary communal expressions of faith and forms of prayer. As monks and nuns, our concern is the adoration of God more than putting on a performance that will inspire visitors. If we spend time making our liturgical prayer beautiful and meaningful, we do so not simply for the sake of aesthetic enjoyment but for the honor and glory of God. Monastic liturgical prayer can be enjoyable, beautiful, reverent, and spiritually nourishing without sacrificing simplicity or making simplicity an end in itself.

Experience teaches us that we can pray and praise God even when the liturgy is not materially perfect, as long as the rendition is correct enough to avoid becoming a major distraction. Yet an aesthetically beautiful rendition may be a powerful stimulus to our inward attitude of devotion in spirit and in truth, just as a slipshod liturgy may provoke frustration.

We want to keep in mind that, as the Second Vatican Council explains, "The liturgy is the summit toward which the activity of the Church is directed; at the same time it is the font from which all her power flows" (SC 10). The liturgy has a central and normative place, though not necessarily an exclusive place, in our monastic life. In addition to liturgical prayer, monks and nuns also practice meditation and sacred reading, self-discipline, the moral virtues, hospitality, loving service of others, and apostolic works. In most monasteries the daily timetable is articulated around the Office and Mass so that everything centers on worship.

---

entirely to divine worship in the contemplative life or have legitimately undertaken some apostolate or work of Christian charity" (Second Vatican Council, *Perfectae Caritatis* [Decree on the Appropriate Renewal of Religious Life], 9, http://www.vatican.va/archive/hist_councils/ii_vatican_council/documents/vat-ii_decree_19651028_perfectae-caritatis_en.html. The original text of the key phrase is *sive in umbratili vita integre se divino cultui dedicent*).

Worshipping Community

Worship finds expression not only in liturgical prayer but also in the framework of our entire monastic life. A sense of the sacred underpins our daily activities and manifests itself in reverence, silence, gentleness, courtesy, and general harmony. Here we consider three traditional monastic themes that illustrate the prayerful, devotional aspect of our monastic communities, namely, the community as priestly people and as bride of Christ and the monastery as the city of God.

Priestly People. Apart from the sacrament of orders received by some monks, we all have a share in the priesthood of Christ by reason of our baptism. Christ as priest offers a pleasing worship to his eternal Father. The First Letter of Peter calls the faithful "a chosen race, a royal priesthood, a holy nation, a people of his own, so that you may announce the praises of him who called you out of darkness into his wonderful light" (1 Pet 2:9-10). Our indelible baptismal character commissions us to participate actively in the church's liturgical worship. As a priestly people we have a spiritual worship to offer God. Saint Paul says: "I urge you therefore, brothers, by the mercies of God, to offer your bodies as a living sacrifice, holy and pleasing to God, your spiritual worship" (Rom 12:1). The worshipping community offers living sacrifices that are holy and acceptable to God, the offering of ourselves sealed on the day of our solemn profession, the sacrifice of our whole life lived out in daily service of our brothers and sisters in a spirit of faith, hope, and love. When we gather for formal liturgical prayer, our ritual is not mere formalism, because we bring to it an active attitude of worship in mind and heart, a free personal response and involvement. When we go to choir or celebrate Eucharist together, we try to put our whole selves in harmony with our words and acts. Saint Benedict calls for precisely such harmony (see RB 19.7).

Bride of Christ. Vatican II invoked the biblical metaphor of the bride to describe the dialogical nature of the Divine Office, calling it "truly the voice of the bride addressed to her bridegroom" (SC 84). Monks and nuns can recognize themselves as the bride of Christ, feminine before him, precious in his eyes, chosen and

loved by him. As a worshipping community we carry on a liturgical dialogue of love with our divine bridegroom in an alternation
of call and response, listening and answering. The Lord speaks
his word, and the community responds in praise, thanksgiving,
intercession, repentance, and songs of joy and gladness. In the
liturgical interaction, the bridegroom sanctifies his bride, cleans-
ing us by the washing of water with the word and preparing us
for the wedding, "that he might present to himself the church in
splendor, without spot or wrinkle or any such thing" (Eph 5:27).
The wedding itself will be celebrated in the kingdom of heaven
(Rev 19:7-8). In this life the bride is always somehow separated
from her Bridegroom, seeking him, calling to him. "The Spirit
and the bride say, 'Come.' Let the hearer say, 'Come'" (Rev 22:17).
The Song of Songs uses the imagery of lover and beloved calling to each other and seeking each other in a playful dialogue:
"Where do you shepherd, where do you give rest at midday?
. . . I called out after him but he did not answer me" (Song 1:7,
5:6). The monastic community as a worshipping community has
a bridal, covenantal, dialogical relationship with the Lord that
puts life into liturgical prayer.

City of God. In the twelfth century, some Cistercian and Benedictine monasteries numbered hundreds of residents and had
many large buildings to accommodate them, plus workshops,
gardens, and livestock to support them. Monasteries were miniature cities. In our day, although a monastery's buildings may
be numerous and large, the residents usually are not numerous.
Nevertheless, because of its purpose, there is a sense in which
every monastery can be a city of God, even a new Jerusalem,
evoking the psalmist's jubilation: "I rejoiced when they said to
me, 'Let us go to the house of the LORD.' And now our feet are
standing within your gates, Jerusalem!" (Ps 122:1-2).

In the monastic Jerusalem, God dwells with his people; we
are God's people, and God is always with us (Rev 21:3). Scripture speaks of two Jerusalems, the earthly and the heavenly. In
monastic liturgical prayer the two cities converge. Just as the
earthly Jerusalem was the place where God was continually worshipped in solemn liturgy and daily sacrifice according to the

model Moses had been shown on the mountain, so the monastic community is a place where the liturgy is celebrated day and night. In contrast to the monastic city, whole sections of some large cities in the world today are inhospitable, overcrowded, and loud, with polluted air and streets and sidewalks strewn with litter. In the cloisters and choirs of monastic cities, a spirit of life and beauty usually prevails—a spirit of celebration, with singing, processions, security, and good company.[2]

The Church at Prayer

Jesus promised "where two or three are gathered together in my name, there am I in the midst of them" (Matt 18:20). Whenever the monastic community is gathered together for prayer, the whole Church is gathered, with Jesus in their midst. From earliest times, whenever Christians came together, they prayed. We are told that after the ascension of Jesus, the apostles gathered in the upper room where they were staying and "devoted themselves with one accord to prayer, together with some women, and Mary the mother of Jesus, and his brothers" (Acts 1:14). Their common prayer was the fountain from which all their action flowed. When we understand that the monastic community gathered in liturgical prayer manifests the universal Church in prayer, we can understand why Saint Benedict tells us that "nothing is to be preferred to the Work of God [*opus Dei*]" (RB 43.3). It is our privilege as well as our duty to manifest the Church at prayer.

Not only is the universal Church present at our liturgical prayer, but the material universe itself is there. With some practice we can be attentive to this cosmic dimension. The connections are to be found in the furnishings of the church, such as the wood of the choir stalls or the crucifix, the beeswax in the candles, the holy water, the incense, the fabric of vestments and altar cloths. The connections are strongest in the eucharistic bread and wine, fruit of the earth, fruit of the vine. Through these natural elements

---

[2] See Thomas Merton, *Love and Living* (New York: Farrar, Straus and Giroux, 1979), 50–53.

as through the roots of a tree, the Church at prayer reaches down into materiality and lifts it up to "share in the glorious freedom of the children of God" (Rom 8:21). Our liturgical prayer helps to transform all created reality.

The transforming effects of liturgical prayer also overflow to the monks and nuns in the choir stalls who are offering their prayers to the greater glory of God. The glory we give to God comes back to us a hundredfold. The liturgical prayer of the Eucharist and the Divine Office is nourishment for our spiritual life, although the result is not automatic or without effort on our part. Cooperation with grace is crucial. Our mind and heart, not just our voice, need to be involved in what we are doing. Saint Benedict's advice is on the mark here: "Let your mind be in harmony with your voice" (RB 19.7). That is to say, be attentive, be focused, try to avoid daydreaming and drowsiness. Put your whole heart into liturgical prayer in the presence of Jesus, and your heart will catch fire within you, like the two disciples on the way to Emmaus who said, "Were not our hearts burning while he spoke to us on the way and opened the scriptures to us?" (Luke 24:32).

Praying with the Whole Self

When Saint Benedict called for psalmody that harmonized both mind and voice, he was evoking a type of prayer that springs not only from the soul but also from the body, that is, prayer with the whole self. Good liturgy works in ways perceptible to our bodily senses as well as to our intellect (SC 7). A liturgy that is predominantly verbal is communicating predominantly to people's heads, to rational, analytical processes, instead of to the whole self.

A human being takes in spiritual nourishment through the senses as well as through the intellect. In addition to words and music that enter us through our ears, the liturgy may employ candles, incense, banners, flowers, choir garments, and vestments of various colors. The body is further involved in gestures, movement, and postures such as standing, sitting, kneeling, bowing, and turning. All these go together in prayer that involves the whole self.

We can appreciate the reason for praying with one's whole self, body and soul, when we understand what it means to be a human being. A human person is not essentially a disembodied soul that happens to be housed for a short span of years in a mortal body that someday will be sloughed off. A living human person is a body-spirit unity, a body enlivened by spirit and a spirit incarnate in flesh. I cannot say that I am essentially my body or that I am essentially my spirit. I am at the same time an embodied spirit and an inspirited body. As believers in the immortality of the soul and the resurrection of the body, we understand that body and soul belong together. What is deepest in me my body can express only with inarticulate sounds (Rom 8:26) or with silence (see Rev 8:1).

The sacraments celebrate our redemption in body and spirit; in the sacraments our whole self encounters and contacts the risen body of Christ.[3] The encounter takes place through the interaction of persons and by means of material, corporeal elements. The grace received in the sacraments permeates the entire body-spirit self, promoting bodily health and sowing the seed of the future glory of the resurrection. Before communicating, the priest prays in the Mass for "protection in mind and body and a healing remedy."

The Divine Office likewise is a celebration involving both mind and body. We begin with a bodily gesture that can set the tone for the whole Office—a sign of the cross made as we sing, "O God, come to my assistance." The more thoughtfully, carefully, and reverently we perform this simple gesture, the easier it is to maintain the inward devotion we express. Even without accompanying words or thoughts, gesture itself can be pure prayer. When we bow profoundly and reverently on entering the church, we pray. When we sit silently and attentively during the pause after the reading of the word of God, we pray.

It may even be possible to see a rudimentary form of liturgical dance in our simple choir movements, bowing, turning, sitting,

---

[3] See Ambrose Verheul, "Liturgy and the Bodily State," chap. 6 in *Introduction to the Liturgy* (Wheathampstead [Hertfordshire]: Anthony Clarke, 1972).

standing. Although the notion of religious dance is somewhat foreign to Western, postindustrial society, dancing occurs sponta-neously in many cultures as part of their desire to place the body totally at the service of the Lord. King David, an heir of Semitic culture, leaped and danced before the ark. "Give praise with tambourines and dance," cried the sacred poet in the psalter's final summons to praise (Ps 150:4). This psalmist called on all the musical instruments—lyre and harp, strings and pipe and clashing cymbals—to join the dancers: "Let everything that has breath give praise to the Lord!" (Ps 150:6). Our own monastic liturgies are usually more restrained and sedate, but to speak of the choreography of the Divine Office is not far-fetched.

Divine Office

In this section I will examine the structure of the Divine Of-fice with special attention to its dialogical character of call and response.[4] The dialogue takes place between the two sides of choir, and between the word of God and each individual as well as between God and the community as a whole. The interplay between call and response begins even before the Office, when the bell rings and the community responds "with utmost speed, yet with gravity" (RB 43.1).

When all are assembled in the choir stalls, the one who presides initiates the dialogue with God on behalf of all: "O God, come to my assistance!" The response of the choir, "O Lord, make haste to help me," commits each person individually to the communal work of praise and petition, with the assistance of divine grace. The opening hymn of praise strikes a lyrical highpoint and may introduce the theme of the Office or the liturgical season.

An antiphon introduces the psalmody and is repeated after the psalmody as an inclusion. Primarily a transitional element, the antiphon may relate the psalm to the feast day or draw attention to one of its verses. More will be said about the psalmody, but as

---

[4] I rely partly on Maurice Coste, "The Office: A Dynamic Dialogue," *Liturgy O.C.S.O.* (Gethsemani Abbey, Trappist, Kentucky) 11 (October 1977): 97–100.

an element of dialogue, the psalms are God's word appropriated as our word of prayer. The psalms are the doorway through which, along with countless pilgrims before us, we enter the ongoing action of salvation history. The psalms record the story of God's saving works, and we ourselves, as we tell that sacred story, become part of it and speak of our own life history and destiny. These minutes of psalmody engage us with God's word in an active, participative way and prepare us for a more receptive, listening mode of encounter in the reading that follows.

The reading, whether of a scriptural or nonscriptural text, can be heard as God's word to me here and now, just as in sacred reading I receive the word with an attentive, listening heart, a heart of flesh. Whether it is a word of comfort or of warning or of instruction, I submit to it so that I may live by it (see Matt 4:4). The reader at Office and at the Eucharist is a servant of the word; he or she has the responsibility of preparing and delivering the reading effectively. As Benedictine theologian Patrick Regan has said, "Reading at liturgy must be a ministerial act in which a human being embodies God's word and serves it to the faithful so that they in turn may embody it and be brought to life—all living together in the one living word."[5]

The reading stops, but the listener's personal encounter with the word continues in silent reflection. The period of silence is not an empty interlude but a prayerful assimilation of the word. Depending on my inspiration I may use this time for adoration, thanksgiving, petition, compunction, or I may simply remain in the presence of the silent word, communing on a deeper level than by specific acts of prayer. An adequate length of time is needed to make this silent reflection fruitful. At some monasteries, the period of silence at Compline serves as the evening examination of conscience, and the Compline reading is selected to provide matter for examination.

---

[5] Patrick Regan, "Liturgy and the Experience of Celebration," *Worship* 47 (December 1973): 598. See Saint Benedict: "No one should presume to read or sing unless he is able to benefit the hearers; let this be done with humility, seriousness and reverence" (RB 47.3-4).

The silent period of personal response to God's word is followed by one or more elements of verbal, sung response by the community, such as a responsorial psalm or a canticle from the Bible. The response expresses praise, gratitude, and a commitment to live by God's word in our daily life. Corresponding to the hymn at the beginning, the canticle gives us a second lyrical climax. A litany of petition follows, calling to mind the needs of the community, our absent brothers or sisters, and all humanity. The concluding prayer may be the Lord's Prayer, which says everything, and/or a special collect that focuses on one or two specific petitions. In a brief, final dialogue, the superior dismisses the assembly with God's blessing, and we leave blessing the Lord, that he may bless us.

The Psalms

The psalms are the heart of the Divine Office. The Psalter is both our book of prayers and our school of prayer; the more we grasp the deepest meaning of these inspired prayers and make them our own personal prayer, the more our minds are lifted up to God and our hearts opened to God's saving power. How do we pray the psalms in an intimate way? How do we sing them in such a way that, according to John Cassian, they seem to be our very own prayer, composed by us at that moment in response to our own needs?[6] How can we harmonize our heart with our voice so that we will not be honoring God with our lips only, while our hearts are far from him (RB 19.7 and Isa 29:13)?

We are already doing the most important thing by daily interacting with the psalms. Besides meeting them in liturgical prayer, we can occasionally take the psalms as matter for our private sacred reading in order to become even more familiar with them.

---

[6] John Cassian, *Conferences* 10.11, trans. Boniface Ramsey, Ancient Christian Writers no. 57 (Mahwah, NJ: Paulist Press, 1997), 384. Cassian adds: "When we have the same disposition in our heart with which each psalm was sung or written down, then we shall become like its author, grasping its significance beforehand rather than afterward" (384).

Saint Benedict presupposes that all know the psalter by heart (RB 8.3). If this effort seems beyond the ability of modern memories, we can at least learn a few of our favorite psalms by heart, so that they can be our companions at free moments during the day. Experience proves the truth of the ancient saying, "A psalm always on the lips, Christ always in the heart."[7] It is by continual use of the psalms, or phrases from them, as our personal prayers that we become attuned to them and grow to savor them.

There are psalms to resonate with all our moods and emotions. If the Divine Office puts a psalm of praise on our lips when we are feeling depressed, it helps expand our horizon beyond the narrow limits of our present difficulty. The history of God's chosen people, with all its ups and downs, is retold in the psalter. The psalter helped the early Christian community find the vocabulary in which to reflect on the mystery of Jesus, because the Messiah is in the psalms also. We may even read our own life story in the psalms as in a mirror that reflects what we have been, what we now experience, and what we aspire to. We can pray the psalms in the name of the Church, in the name of Christ, and as expressions of our own living relationship with the Lord.

Some amount of earnest study using the best contemporary biblical scholarship is almost a prerequisite for a full appreciation of the Psalter. The psalms can then be understood according to the main themes they express, their historical origins in the period of the Second Temple of Jerusalem, their liturgical use, and their various levels of literal and symbolic interpretation. Some monks and nuns may have the inclination to learn biblical Hebrew so that they can read the psalms in the original or at least in an interlinear version. The rhythm of oral poetry and the nuances of verbal tenses are often obscured in translations.

Even with all these helps, praying the psalms may be difficult. Our attention will wander off in daydreams and fantasies. Distractions during psalmody have been an occupational hazard for monks and nuns since the beginning of monasticism. From

---

[7] Phrase used in a description of Saint Wulfstan, the eleventh-century bishop of Worcester, as found in William of Malmesbury, *Life of St. Wulstan*.

the Desert Father Evagrius we find this frank admission: "A great thing indeed—to pray without distraction; a greater thing still—to sing psalms without distraction."[8] Keeping the quantity of psalms in the Office relatively small may improve the quality of our prayer and encourage a recitation that is leisurely and reflective instead of rushed and distracted. The psalm-tone melody, if it is simple and lyrical, may have a prayerful, meditative effect. The young David soothed King Saul with his lyre and psalmody. A Cistercian nun has observed: "The melody gives the psalm text a chance to dig its way rhythmically, vocally, temporally, into the heart—a way of grace, a way of experience of God."[9]

Choral psalmody can lead to the kind of experience of God that the fifth-century monastic reporter John Cassian called "fiery prayer," prayer with fiery ardor: "Sometimes, while we have been singing, the verse of some psalm has offered the occasion for fiery prayer."[10] As we saw when discussing contemplation as the highest stage of sacred reading, such experiences are the fruit of grace and not the result of our own effort, nor the automatic result of a spirited and aesthetically beautiful rendition of the Divine Office. Cassian, however, is a good witness to the fact that communal liturgical prayer fosters and does not prevent the contemplative encounter with God.

---

[8] Evagrius Ponticus, *Praktikos* 69, in *Praktikos and Chapters on Prayer*, trans. John Eudes Bamberger, CS 4 (Kalamazoo, MI: Cistercian Publications, 1970), 35.

[9] Étienne of Pradines, "Psallite Sapienter," *Liturgy O.C.S.O.* 11 (January 1977): 77. The title of this article, from Ps 46:8, connotes "sing with understanding and skill and spiritual savor," alluding to the savory knowledge of God that is wisdom.

Singing the psalms together in choir can be a subjectively satisfying, even exhilarating, experience that turns us totally to the Lord. Writing of her happy memories of choral singing, April Oursler Armstrong has said, "To sing you use your body, your mind, and your heart. You are committed, engaged, caught up totally. . . . When you sing in a choir, blending your own song into a wholeness with others, there's a glory and a delight which can be real recreation" (*House with a Hundred Gates* [New York: McGraw Hill, 1965], 71). Another approach to the psalmody finds delight simply in listening to the words of a solo psalmist.

[10] Cassian, *Conferences* 9.26, p. 346.

Praying the psalms fruitfully in choir depends on one's style of life outside choir. We cannot expect the savory knowledge of God while we chant the psalms if we neglect searching for God the rest of the day. In his commentary on Psalm 146, Saint Augustine made the point that it is not enough for the mind to be in harmony with the voice; a person's works have to be in harmony as well. As we live, so we pray and so we sing the psalms.

The Eucharist

The Eucharist is the summit of liturgical prayer. There, more powerfully than anywhere else, we meet the Risen Christ present in the fullness of his saving power, bestowing his life-giving grace on the assembled community of worshippers and on his entire body, that is, the Church spread throughout the cosmos and the eons. The Eucharist commemorates, transtemporally, the saving death and resurrection of Jesus—"Do this in memory of me" (Luke 22:19). Finally, the Eucharist, celebrated continually "until he comes" (1 Cor 11:26), foreshadows the final assembly of the redeemed in the kingdom of God. Present, past, and future are bridged in the ritual of the Eucharist.

This is not the place for a theological or liturgical commentary on the Eucharist. Our concern here is to reflect on the value of the eucharistic celebration in our monastic life as the pattern of our own spiritual transformation. The Eucharist deserves to be appreciated as the source of our life in the Spirit. In the liturgy of the Eucharist we make present and actual in our midst the mystery of Christ: "Jesus Christ is the same yesterday, today, and forever" (Heb 13:8). The Paschal Mystery of Christ's life, death, resurrection, and ascension is a blueprint for our own lives. Jesus draws us ever deeper into his mystery and communicates divine life to us according to the pattern of his own life. As we celebrate the Eucharist we permit ourselves to be loved, saved, sanctified, and conformed more completely to the image of Christ.

The spiritual life of Christians follows the arc of Christ's life, through his victorious death, then back to the Father in his risen glory. Each fruitful participation in the liturgy of the Eucharist moves us further along the invisible pathway that passes from the Father who created us, along the way of the cross and resurrection marked out by the Son, and back to the Father by the power of the indwelling Spirit who has been given to us.

Through Jesus Christ, in the Spirit, we come from the Father and return to the Father. At the center of the process of our sanctification and redemption, at the center of the Eucharist and all liturgical prayer, stands the figure of Jesus crucified and risen—the mystery of Christ. The Paschal Mystery is the good news that Paul spoke about so eloquently, the Gospel that we are to preach by our lives (see 1 Tim 3:16; Phil 2:5-11; Col 1:15-20). The Paschal Mystery is also our own passage, our crossing over from spiritual and physical death to the fullness of life in God. Monks and nuns, by their baptismal vocation as well as their religious vocation, reproduce in their own lives the pattern first traced by Christ, until they are conformed to Christ to the glory of God our Father.

In a strikingly apt formula, theologian Cipriano Vagaggini, OSBCam, speaks of the liturgy as "the paschalization of the world, effected by Christ the Lord . . . in the progressive assimilation of the world to Himself."[11] The leading edge of this process of universal paschalization is the eucharistic liturgy. There the living Christ is personally present and acting. To a degree that mysteriously corresponds to our faith and love, he communicates and shares with us his own risen life by leading us through death to resurrection under the veil of material signs. Saint Benedict's vision of the monastic vocation, as we find it expressed at the end of his Prologue, could be summarized in the word "paschalization." Saint Benedict invited his followers, through patience, to "share in the sufferings of Christ that we may deserve also to share in his kingdom" (RB Prol. 50).

Even in our day, amid a diversity of spiritualities, monks and nuns will scarcely be able to find anything more central than this on which to base their entire monastic life. The Paschal Mystery

---

[11] Cipriano Vagaggini, *Theological Dimensions of the Liturgy*, trans. Leonard J. Doyle and W. J. Jurgens (Collegeville, MN: Liturgical Press, 1977), 721.

is fundamental to Christian life. Only by letting go, by dying, do we attain the fullness of life. We see this law verified again and again in our own life, in the lives of those around us, and even in the history of our monastic community. There is no other way to the Father than by the way of Christ crucified and risen. It is in the Eucharist that we encounter this mystery under its most efficacious and dramatic signs. When monastic life centers on the mystery of Christ in the eucharistic celebration, an incredible force of transformation and vitality is released in the community and the daily life of each individual.

Other Devotions

Should our devotional life be nourished by sources other than the Eucharist and the Divine Office? What place in monastic life should be assigned to such popular devotions as the rosary, novenas, Stations of the Cross, litanies, and devotion to Mary and to other saints? These devotions are to be commended and seen as complementary to liturgical prayer, though their value is secondary because they are not the official communal worship of the Church. It could be said, however, that such devotions ordinarily have no place as communal monastic exercises. The prayer of the monastic community is liturgical prayer—celebration of the Mass and Divine Office, plus eucharistic rituals such as Benediction and adoration of the Blessed Sacrament. If the community's liturgy is a living, flexible, adaptable reality, it will furnish adequate forms of expression for the faith experience of most members of the community.

When an individual cannot express his or her experience of faith fully enough in communal liturgical prayer, he or she might seek alternate forms of prayer in private extraliturgical devotions or in faith sharing within small groups. Newcomers to monastic life, who may have found great personal satisfaction in following the spirituality of a particular saint or in certain pious practices and prayers, will probably find the community's liturgical prayer dry and even boring at first. It takes time, repetition, some study, and constant good will to learn to savor the biblical and patristic spirituality at the heart of the Divine Office and Eucharist. This spirituality focuses attention not on the worshipper and his or her subjective feelings but on God who is worshipped and on Jesus Christ, whose life of obedient love is brought before the worshipper in its different mysteries in the course of the liturgical year. Gradually the newcomer will learn to find in communal liturgical prayer the deepest expression of his or her personal relationship with the Lord and will learn to pray the Eucharist and the Divine Office with both mind and heart.

All this does not mean that liturgical prayer must be the only expression of a person's piety. Rosary devotions, devotion to Mary, Stations of the Cross may continue but without being primary in a person's spiritual life. Besides liturgical prayer, we are faithful to sacred reading, to short prayers said during the course of the day, to periods of meditative prayer, and to the call of active, loving service in our daily life. "The spiritual life," says Vatican II, "is not limited solely to participation in the liturgy" (SC 12).[12]

Conclusion

There is a correlation between the quality of our monastic community life and the quality of our liturgical prayer. Life and prayer are intertwined, mutually influencing one another. If there is disharmony and a worldly spirit in the community, members will find it impossible to celebrate liturgy together in a climate of joy, peace, and fellowship. Good liturgical prayer flows from and also contributes to good community. Liturgy, especially the Mass, can strengthen the bonds of community and fraternal charity. Because it looks forward to the coming kingdom of God, the liturgy tends to foster the loving unity that will characterize the community of believers when God has become "all in all" (1 Cor 15:28).

---

[12] On popular devotions Vatican II said: "These devotions should be so drawn up that they harmonize with the liturgical seasons, accord with the sacred liturgy, are in some fashion derived from it, and lead the people to it, since, in fact, the liturgy by its very nature far surpasses any of them" (SC 13).

The test of the genuineness of our liturgical prayer as individuals is not our performance during the Eucharist and Divine Office, and still less our theoretical understanding of liturgy, but the practice of our daily monastic life. The test is not how we behave in church but how we behave outside the church, and in particular how we relate to those whom we meet and with whom we interact during the course of the day. Do we see them as one with us in Christ, called as we are to offer blessing, honor, glory, and dominion to God forever and ever (Rev 5:13-14)? Do we stop to help a brother or sister in need or do we pass by, saying that the bell for Office is about to ring and we cannot be late? Do we show others the forbearance, gentleness, patience, and cheerfulness that are continually exemplified in the lives of the saints we commemorate throughout the year? Liturgical prayer is designed to lead us ever deeper into the mystery of Christ until we live not for ourselves but for him who died for all humanity and rose again (2 Cor 5:15). Learning the full meaning of liturgical prayer and being transformed by it will occupy us for a lifetime.

Questions for Reflection

How can the psalms be meaningful to Christians when the psalms are steeped in violence and never mention Jesus Christ?

If there are too few in choir for the satisfactory celebration of the Divine Office, what are some alternatives?

i set you over kingdoms and nations to tear up and knock down,

to destroy and to overthrow, to build and to plant

WORK

We come now to the third major element in the triadic structure of monastic life—work. A portion of almost every day will be spent in performing some sort of service for the monastic community or the larger ecclesial community. Benedictines have taken on ministries in a variety of fields—education, health care, parish ministry, and foreign missions, to name a few. The Trappist-Cistercian tradition has favored farm work, animal husbandry, and, in modern times, small industries.

By our work we intend to accomplish something good for others or ourselves. Without this intention of doing something useful, we are simply playing, not working. When monks and nuns work they tend to put themselves wholeheartedly into their task and to accomplish it fairly well. They take pride in their creative accomplishments and rightly so. Without the sense of personal creative involvement, work becomes a dreary effort. Putting these elements together, we may describe monastic work, in general, as creative effort for useful purposes.[1] Our work is

---

[1] See "Drudgery, Play and Work," *Good Work: Catholic Art Association Bulletin* (Winter 1964): 3.

sometimes weighted on the side of toil and sometimes on the side of play. Most of the time our work is in between, with a sprinkling of both toil and play. Monastic work shares the universal reality of human labor: partly enjoyable, partly tedious, but always inevitable.

As I reflect in this chapter on aspects of monastic work, circling around the subject so as to observe more facets of it, I will try to recall the perspective reached in the chapters on sacred reading and liturgical prayer. These three monastic practices need to flow into and out of one another if our day is to have a character of wholeness and simplicity instead of being a succession of disjointed, unrelated segments. Work joins prayer and sacred reading in an integrated and well-balanced monastic life. If work is entirely missing, or stressed to the exclusion of liturgical prayer and sacred reading, the imbalance eventually will be felt.

Work and Values

In discussing work, the Desert Fathers and Mothers often referred to the instruction and example of Saint Paul, a tentmaker by trade. To the Thessalonians Paul wrote, "In toil and drudgery, night and day we worked, so as not to burden any of you. . . . In fact, when we were with you, we instructed you that if anyone was unwilling to work, neither should that one eat" (2 Thess 3:7-10). The monks of Egypt refused to rely for their support on alms and donations, even from relatives. Instead, they felt obliged to earn their bread by their own labor. Their work also enabled them to distribute surplus food to pilgrims or prisoners or the famine stricken.[2]

Experience soon taught the desert monks and nuns that manual labor offered a distinct value to the spiritual life. If they attempted to give themselves totally to reading and prayers, they became restless, wanted to know about other people's affairs, indulged in gossip and idle conversation, made envious comparisons and

---

[2] See John Cassian on "The Spirit of Acedia," *Institutes* 10.22, in *The Institutes*, Ancient Christian Writers 58 (New York: The Newman Press, 2000), 233.

generally lost their purity of heart and their attention to God.[3]
If, however, they kept their hands occupied with a simple, even
monotonous, task, they could more easily keep their mind and
heart centered on God for long periods of time. Thus, in order
to avoid idleness, they preferred to work.[4]

Not all kinds of work, however, were equally appropriate.
Basket weaving was considered appropriate, or a small garden
wrested from the desert waste, but not large-scale agricultural
projects. One of the reasons that these seekers went to the desert
instead of to arable regions was so that "the quality of a rich soil
will never move us to the distraction of some kind of farming,
by which our mind might be drawn away from the principle of
the heart and be too worn out for spiritual pursuits."[5] Primary in
the interests of the Desert Fathers and Mothers was their spiritual
aim; the nature and extent of their involvement in work was
determined ultimately by their spiritual aim.

Was Saint Benedict's idea of monastic work different from that
of the Desert Fathers and Mothers described by Cassian? Benedict
was legislating for communities rather than for hermits, and so he
was obliged to face the economic reality of supporting a community. Work places tended to multiply as the community increased
in size. The Rule envisioned a monastery in which "water, mill
and garden are contained, and the various crafts are practiced"
(RB 66.6), where products of these artisans may be sold (RB 57.4),
a place surrounded by fields whose crops had to be harvested

---

[3] Cassian, "The Spirit," 222–24.

[4] Some who did not need extra work still worked. Abba Paul had an
ample supply of food from some date palms and a small garden, but he also
imposed on himself the labor of weaving baskets. "He used to collect palm
fronds and always exact a day's labor from himself just as if this were his
means of support. And when his cave was filled with a whole year's work,
he would burn up what he had so carefully toiled over each year. . . . And
so, although the obligation of earning a livelihood did not demand this
course of action, he did it just for the sake of purging his heart, firming his
thoughts, persevering in his cell, and conquering and driving out acedia"
(Cassian, *Institutes*, 10.24, 233).

[5] John Cassian, *Conferences* 24.12, trans. Boniface Ramsey, Ancient Christian
Writers no. 57 (Mahwah, NJ: Paulist Press, 1997), 835.

(RB 48.7). Nevertheless, Benedict shared the desert view of work as valuable in order to avoid idleness, "the enemy of the soul" (RB 48.1), and for the support of the community. Saint Benedict's major statement on work as a means of self-support occurs in his chapter on the daily horarium: "They must not become distressed if local conditions or their poverty should force them to do the harvesting themselves. When they live by the labor of their hands, as our fathers and the apostles did, then they are really monks. Yet all things are to be done with moderation on account of the fainthearted" (RB 48.7-9).[6]

By setting specific limits to the time spent daily in manual labor, Benedict hoped to prevent work from becoming the dominant concern of his disciples at the expense of their spiritual aim. Monastic work was not to have priority over God's work of liturgical prayer: "On hearing the signal for an hour of the divine office the monk will immediately set aside what he has in hand and go with utmost speed, yet with gravity and without giving occasion for frivolity" (RB 43.1-2). A Cistercian monk, Anthony Hayes, has observed, "This point is stressed and undoubtedly points to the relative unimportance of finishing any particular job."[7]

If monastic work is to retain its value as a means and not become an end in itself, the Benedictine balance of work, sacred reading, and liturgical prayer needs to be maintained, though not necessarily in the proportions of Saint Benedict's original timetable. The balance seems to be increasingly threatened in our time as apostolic commitments, the proliferation of meetings, and important economic realities become more pressing. Already in the twelfth century the Cistercians discovered that they could not support themselves in a feudal, agricultural economy without the help of lay brothers or lay sisters, who spent longer hours in manual work so that the choir religious might be free for choir, sacred reading, or other forms of work.

---

[6] *The Rule of St. Benedict 1980*, ed. Timothy Fry (Collegeville, MN: Liturgical Press, 1981), 253.

[7] Anthony Hayes, "Manual Work: Another Look at its Role in Cistercian Life," *Hallel* 3 (Winter 1976): 181. Elsewhere the author's emphasis differs from my own.

In our own time, in a postindustrial, technological age, further creative thinking is needed to maintain a balanced monastic way of life. This is not the place to attempt solutions to problems of self-support in the face of rising expenses, inflation, taxation, insufficient personnel, aging communities, or demands for higher standards of living. The trend in many cases has been to seek solutions along the lines of higher productivity through advanced technology and careful planning. Modern monks and nuns have become dependent on machines and technology to do the work once accomplished by hand. In this way we have been able to meet our commitments and still preserve sufficient leisure time for sacred reading and liturgical prayer. Technology, however, has brought problems of its own: costly acquisition, maintenance, and repair of equipment, accelerated pace of living and working, concomitant psychological pressure and stress, assembly-line boredom, and increased contacts with society.

In our contemporary situation, what values can we preserve in monastic work? Can our work still serve the spiritual aims of monastic life? The question needs to be answered in terms that can apply to a wide range of tasks from intellectual and apostolic ministries to manual labor of all types. Ultimately each member of the community has the problem of working out a personal relationship with his or her own job, so that this daily occupation is seen as somehow valuable and ennobling.

People who visit a monastery should find a community of men or women who are relaxed and happy in their work, not a group of tense, driven souls subsisting on tranquilizers. A healthy attitude toward work is part of the witness we can offer to the world today. Our Benedictine forefathers taught methods of agriculture to the barbarian tribes of northern Europe. Perhaps one of the civilizing roles of monks and nuns today might be to give the world an example of how to employ technology while retaining our humanity.[8]

---

[8] Margaret Mary Hanron makes this point effectively: "Far from changing the rhythm of our life into one determined by technology, the assembly-line routine, etc., it is more than ever necessary for us to be able to avail ourselves

Monasteries might demonstrate how persons can use modern mechanization and automation without being dominated and dehumanized by it. The fascinating world of science and technology dominates human beings and becomes their idol when they forget that human hands and minds have fashioned these machines and can remain in control of them. Another role that monks and nuns might fulfill is to take responsibility for the short-term and long-term effects of human intervention in the processes of nature and the fertility of the land. Perhaps monks and nuns can be examples of the restrained and prudent use of traditional and alternative forms of energy. In an age when people can scarcely think except in terms of the largest possible scale, the fastest, most powerful, most up-to-date, most expensive possibilities, monasteries might give witness to the value of what is more manageable, poorer, more compatible with the deeper needs of the human spirit.[9] In a society where some workers consider work merely a necessary evil and would prefer to live on welfare or stock dividends, monks and nuns can be examples of motivated workers who find in their tasks a genuine fulfillment as human beings.

Monastic work in modern society serves all these values as well as the ancient monastic values of self-support, hospitality, and avoidance of idleness. Saint Benedict affirms the transcendent value and goal of monastic work in his instruction on selling the goods produced by the abbey. He suggests that prices be set not with an eye on maximum profit but with attention to the primary purpose of work, "so that in all things God may be glorified" (RB 57.9, quoting 1 Pet 4:11).

---

of the advantages of technology and mechanization without destroying this human rhythm and balance. To restore this human rhythm, to find a place for a certain amount of contemplative leisure, is the crying need of our times. Those who come to us must find in our life the balance which will bring healing to their own" ("Lectio Divina and Study in St. Bernard and at Present," *Hallel* 1 [November 1974]: 31–32). A video of Cistercian nuns seeking this balance is available at http://www.mississippiabbey.org/Monastic_Work.

[9] The case for productivity as if people mattered is well stated by Ernst F. Schumacher, *Small Is Beautiful* (New York: Perennial Library, 1975). See also the encyclical letter of Pope Francis, *Laudato Si': On Care for Our Common Home*, chap. 3.

Our work is an integral part of our life and partakes in the ultimate value of our whole existence—the greater honor and glory of God. Since monastic life is ordered primarily to God, the various monastic practices all have their value from this transcendent intentionality. Monks and nuns may be doing the same type of work as people outside the abbey, but our motive, attitude, and approach are ultimately religious, and so our work has a religious value. We are working not simply for ourselves or for our monastic family or for the poor; we are working for God. Working for God does not exclude all other values and motives but permeates them and redirects them beyond themselves, toward "a new heaven and a new earth" (Rev 21:1).[10]

Work as Restoration

In the second (or Yahwist) creation story, the earth was in a wild, uncultivated state until the Lord God created a human being "to till the ground" (Gen 2:5). The obligation to work was imposed on humanity in its original state before the Fall. Work belongs to the essential rhythm of a fully human life. It is natural for human beings to want to work, to enjoy working, and to experience the normal satisfaction of a job well done. In the Garden of Eden, harmony reigned until disobedience brought an end to that idyllic world. Sin ruined the harmony between humanity and the natural environment, and work lost its spontaneous, self-perfecting character. Human beings were commanded to work, in accordance with their nature and their need, but their work was now to be burdensome and penitential. The classic biblical instance of work after the Fall is the slave labor of the Israelites in Egypt, forced to make bricks without straw being supplied to them (Exod 5:18).

---

[10] Thomas Merton cautioned that a monk or nun must not work solely for the love and glory of God while forgetting the objective task at hand. We may not work without any care for doing our task responsibly because we are more interested in saying short prayers and perhaps also in getting some fresh air and exercise that would be good for our health. See Thomas Merton, *Monastic Orientation*, Series 5, no. 23, unpublished mimeographed edition (Abbey of Gethsemani, 1950), 72.

Because of the redemptive activity of Jesus and also his own occupation as an obscure carpenter, the condition of human beings as workers has been partially restored to what it was before the Fall. Work has not entirely lost its penitential aspect, because the world still awaits the fullness of its redemption (Rom 8:19), but human work, when it cooperates with the good balance of nature, furthers the process of universal restoration (see Acts 3:21). At Madonna House, a training center for the lay apostolate in Ontario, Canada, where a typically Russian love of the soil prevails, the philosophy behind the farm work is restoration. Working close to the soil, the community is conscious of restoring for human use a rock-strewn strip of land and of restoring themselves and their own humanity in the process. The farm work is intended to humanize their natural surroundings, of which they themselves are a living part, and to produce vegetables and grain to feed their community and the poor of the neighborhood.

Work as restoration respects the harmonious balance between nature's needs and human intervention, and in that way work helps to liberate the world from its bondage to corruption (Rom 8:21). Instead of exercising a brutal, wasteful domination of nature, the worker keeps a careful watch over the delicate ecological balance of life in his or her environment. Humanity as worker is the shepherd of all God's creation, guiding it skillfully but gently toward its share "in the glorious freedom of the children of God" (Rom 8:21). The monastic worker has his or her own small area of responsibility in which to exercise the task of good shepherding. I do my particular part if I can keep order, harmony, and beauty in that one area even though the effort goes unnoticed.

Hiddenness of Monastic Work

Monastic work is often hidden, humble, anonymous, even monotonous. We believe there can be great value in obeying God's will by daily fidelity to our assigned task. Ours is the hidden, obscure life of the poor throughout the world who are inheritors of the role of the lowly ones, called the *anawim* in the Bible. The spirit of the *anawim* was simplicity, littleness, dependence on God. They were unnoticed in the world. Monks and nuns, likewise, have no need to be noticed, even by their brothers or sisters. Instead of seeking spectacular, glamorous jobs, operating the largest and noisiest piece of equipment on the place, we try to content ourselves with whatever job we are assigned, doing what has to be done. To be "hidden with Christ in God" (Col 3:3) is the life we have chosen, or been chosen for. It is the life of everyday routine and quiet, steady accomplishments, like a tree silently growing to maturity. There is not a great deal of fanfare and commotion as a tree grows, but anyone who sees it after a number of years marvels at its height.

However humble and hidden it may be, "in the Lord your labor is not in vain" (1 Cor 15:58). Jesus himself led the hidden life of a small-town carpenter, fashioning things from wood, leather, and metal for the needs of his community. All the while his larger mission was to refashion the hearts of men and women and to build the kingdom of God. Monks and nuns are still laboring to build up the kingdom of God. Whatever we do, little or great, we are doing it for God's kingdom, not for our own prestige and glory, not for our own kingdom.

Yet the little things that are done exceedingly well out of love for God, not for show, do have a power of restoration for the individual monk or nun. The Old Testament story of Elisha's cure of Naaman the leper illustrates the power of ordinary, commonplace actions. Elisha had instructed Naaman to do a simple thing: "Go and wash seven times in the Jordan" (2 Kgs 5:10). Naaman, who had a much more spectacular cure in mind, refused to trifle with meaningless ablutions in the Jordan, saying, "I thought that he would surely come out to me and stand there to call on the name of the Lord his God, and would move his hand over the place, and thus cure the leprous spot. Are not the rivers of Damascus, the Abana and the Pharpar, better than all the waters of Israel?" (2 Kgs 5:11-12). It was only after his servants reasoned with him that Naaman went down and plunged seven times into the Jordan; then his flesh became "like the flesh of a little child," and he was clean (2 Kgs 5:14).

The monk or nun, asked to spend a lifetime doing a succession of little tasks, may be tempted to complain as Naaman did: "I thought there was more to monastic life than this! Why doesn't the abbot give me something more important to do?" God the Creator knows the best way to bring all his creatures to their highest realization. God tells us through superiors to immerse ourselves day after day in the common stream of monastic living—the work, the liturgical prayer, the sacred reading, and all the other monastic practices. If we do them with complete trust, we begin to experience the transforming power of these common ways, and eventually we too are cleansed, restored like a little child. Monastic work in its hiddenness conceals a power for restoring the worker that can be appreciated only by experiencing it.

The human ego, however, resists hiddenness and prefers tangible results, the more spectacular the better. Ego-oriented work is an obstacle to the monastic goal of spiritual restoration. Not all work is spiritually profitable; selfless work offered to the glory of God is. In Hindu tradition, work as a path to God is called Karma Yoga, the path of action. In order to lead to God, the action must be selfless, not motivated by ambition or profit, but an offering made to God. Karma Yoga implies the renunciation of an ego-centeredness that always looks for spectacular results and is dismayed by failure. According to the teaching of the *Bhagavad-Gita*, when my work is free of ego-centeredness I am no longer the doer; instead, my activity flows from an inner center of contemplative rest, and the work is holy because my heart is fixed on God.

Our own Western monastic traditions have stressed the importance of detachment from work. In the monastery we take the work we get and do our task for God, trusting in his assistance. If we are asked to drop what we are about and to do something else for God, we can do so without a mental breakdown or prolonged depression. The failure of a work project does not mean the collapse of our world, because the horizon of our world extends farther than our work project.

Impossible Tasks

Saint Benedict's parallel to the Hindus' Karma Yoga occurs in the chapter on "The Assignment of Impossible Tasks to a Brother." In Benedict's time, a job may have seemed impossible because it was physically difficult, beyond a person's physical strength. Today a job may seem impossible because it appears meaningless and useless. Benedict's recommendation still applies. He advised the monk first to give the job a good try. The next step, if the task still seems impossible, is to take the matter to his superior, but not in a spirit of pride or rebellion. Should the superior persist in the command, even after hearing the monk's honest and tactful explanation of the problem, then the monk is to go back and try again, for love, and "trusting in God's help" (RB 68.5). Benedict pointed out the path of selfless action and renunciation of the ego, but at the same time assured the monk that this meaningless, impossible task would somehow benefit him: "this is best for him" (RB 68.4).

Benedict's doctrine is worth exploring. How can such work be for my good? Perhaps because it teaches me a fundamental fact about myself as worker—that I am dependent on God, who is master of the impossible and source of all meaning. My own strength and creativity are involved in my work, but ultimately, according to the biblical view, I am collaborating with God and dependent on God's creative power to bring about his plan for the universe. "I have the strength for everything through him who empowers me" (Phil 4:13). Human weakness and failure are no obstacles to the divine plan but are included in it. Seemingly impossible or meaningless tasks have their purpose in the divine plan.

In our day some attention is usually given to the monastic worker's preferences and abilities, so that the task does not exceed his or her physical or psychological strength and even provides a certain fulfillment. Still, there will be times when my work assignment seems to me meaningless or impossible. I may feel I am merely putting in time, doing something that does not need to be done. Sickness or old age may lead to a forced retirement and the feeling of being put on the shelf and forgotten, perhaps for years. All this can be painfully demoralizing and a heavy blow to a person's self-esteem. I am given work that seems useless, or given no work at all, with the implication that I am too weak-minded or frail of body to be entrusted with any productive enterprise. How is someone to deal with the feelings that arise when he or she is faced with pointless, useless work?

I have to remember first that my worth as a person does not come from the positions I hold or the tasks I accomplish in life but from who I am as a human being and child of God. I am greater than my work. It is I who give value to my work by doing it for love, and "trusting in God's help" (RB 68.5). Menial tasks acquire dignity from the personal dignity of the worker.[11] Being and doing are two distinct potentialities of my selfhood, and they need to be appreciated in their differences. Being is prior and preeminent to doing. Simply to be, to be fully present with calmness, strength, and freedom, is deeper and more central in me than any activity. Action is secondary and built on the foundation of being. Active doing should not have to substitute for my sense of being and being valuable. I can rest secure and content in the fullness of simply being who I am. I do not need to feel anxious or threatened when my doing side is not called on to actualize its talents. The chief purpose of monastic life, after all, is *not* to do. Making and doing are not as essential as being and seeing and loving.

Monastic life gives us license to be at times creatively inactive and at leisure for God. Contemplation is a functionally useless occupation, a sheer waste of time, but it is also the highest form of creative involvement. Long ago the Roman Stoic philosopher Cato said that "he was never so busy as when he did nothing, and never less solitary than when alone."[12] Doing nothing may

---

[11] John Paul II drew attention to the personal dimension—that is, the worker—as the primary source of the value and dignity of the work being done, in contrast to the objective dimension or kind of work being done (*Laborem Exercens* [September 14, 1981], no. 6).

[12] Attributed to Cato by Cicero, *De Re Publica* 1.17, trans. Francis Barham, http://www.kingsacademy.com/mhodges/08_Classics-Library/hellenist -roman/cicero/de-re-publica/de-re-publica_1.htm.

be harder for us than doing something, but it is not less valuable. In monastic life we can rejoice in our opportunity to do nothing and produce nothing.

Sometimes a mistaken notion of Christian charity leads a monk or nun into the activist trap of doing more and more for others until his or her own personal relationship with the Lord is smothered under a mountain of good deeds. Eventually that person has nothing of worth left to give others because he or she has not taken the time to replenish the reservoir of his or her own spirit. The words of the psalmist are always there to call us back to contemplation: "Be still and know that I am God!" (Ps 46:11).

From another point of view, things we do will always be relatively unimportant if we are to take seriously the saying of Jesus, "We are unprofitable servants; we have done what we were obliged to do" (Luke 17:10). Regardless of how prestigious or how meaningless our job, we have to admit that we are simply doing our duty and deserve no reward. We have nothing to boast of before God. Of ourselves, we are unprofitable servants, and any good we accomplish is due to the power of God working along with and in us.

Work teaches this lesson when, no matter what we do, nothing seems to go right. Monastic manual labor brings us again and again up against the obduracy of things. Things are the way they are, and we have to live with them and work with them as they are. Sometimes we feel we are expected to make something out of nothing, using poor materials and inoperable equipment under the most inopportune working conditions. Failure seems inevitable. At these moments, we taste our own human weakness and have to acknowledge our dependence on God for anything we may accomplish. We have no right to expect everything always to go smoothly and successfully. We can expect only "thorns and thistles" (Gen 3:18), the recalcitrance of reality. Yet we can work with a deep sense of peace, realizing that we are God's unprofitable servants and letting God be our profit, our vindication, our upholder, our all.

Letting go of the urge to manage everything is part of the dying that leads to new life and fruitfulness within the Paschal Mystery. Jesus on the cross was in the position of one who could achieve nothing, who was totally unproductive. With his hands nailed to the cross, he was the picture of absolute powerlessness and uselessness. Nevertheless, simply by being there for love and "trusting in God's help" (RB 68.5), Jesus redeemed the world. He redeemed us more efficaciously when he was powerless on the cross than when he was traveling about, preaching and working miracles. Our work, whatever it may be throughout our life, acquires intrinsic fruitfulness when we accept it as God's will. Faith in the Paschal Mystery aligns our work with Christ's great redemptive work that was his prayer from the cross for the salvation of the world. Saint John Paul II has described how human work may enter into the salvation process: "By enduring the toil of work in union with Christ crucified for us, man in a way collaborates with the son of God for the redemption of humanity."[13]

Workaholism

Work and prayer can converge in monastic life; the point of that convergence is a heart permeated with love. Work and prayer both express love. Self-forgetful service of others is, like prayer, a movement out of myself toward the other, a movement of giving, of love.[14]

"If work can be prayer, why may I not work as much as possible, so as to be praying continually?" Not many monks or nuns would rationalize their intentions so simplistically, but this question might betray their underlying assumptions. In the lives of some of us, work has acquired paramount importance. Our work is all for God, as our life is all for God, but work seems to have become all our life. In moments of honesty and terrible fatigue,

---

[13] John Paul II, *Laborem Exercens* no. 27, http://www.vatican.va/holy _father/john_paul_ii/encyclicals/documents/hf_jp-ii_enc_14091981 _laborem-exercens_en.html. See also Adrian van Kaam, "Working with Jesus," chap. 11 in *Looking for Jesus* (Denville, NJ: Dimension Books, 1978).

[14] Terrence Kardong, OSB, explains that the motto *Ora et Labora* is not in the Rule of Saint Benedict, nor can work be equated with prayer. See "Work Is Prayer: Not!" *Assumption Abbey Newsletter* 23, no. 4 (October 1995), http:// www.osb.org/gen/topics/work/kard1.html.

we may secretly wonder where God is in all this. Is this still the monastic life? Or is it an addiction called workaholism?

Workaholism is legitimate activity carried to an excessive, unhealthy extreme. The term *workaholics* has been given to persons who spend sixty hours or more a week, apart from Sunday, at their jobs: Wall Street analysts, junior bankers, new physicians in residency, farmers getting in the harvest work fifteen hours a day. Outside of work they have no normal life. They are high achievers and are rewarded financially or by positions of power or by fame.[15] These people are motivated by the pleasure they obtain from functioning skillfully in the face of challenges and stress. A rush of adrenaline increases their energy and strength temporarily, but in the long term they face depression and burnout.

Studies show that productivity and efficiency actually diminish after a certain point of overwork: "Among industrial workers, working overtime raises the rate of mistakes and safety mishaps; likewise, for knowledge workers fatigue and sleep-deprivation make it hard to perform at a high cognitive level."[16] Nevertheless, corporations love hard workers. They enable the workaholics on their self-destructive path and even reward them with bonuses that they will never have a chance to spend. Like other forms of addiction, work may bring workaholics to an early death before they have savored the deepest joys of living.

There is a support group for workaholics called "Workaholics Anonymous." Established in the 1980s, it makes use of the twelve-step program. Among the many recommended tools of recovery are listening, playing, and relaxing, living in the now. The principles of recovery include abstaining from the compulsive behavior, taking time out, rediscovering humor, rediscovering meditation, learning how to take it easy. Workaholics might say, "Take it easy," when taking their leave from someone, but

[15] See Loral Graham, "Is the Price of Success Too High?" *Flightime* (December 1975), rpt. from *Atlanta Magazine*, 1975. Ten business executives and their wives are interviewed.

[16] James Surowiecki, "The Cult of Overwork," *The New Yorker* XC, no. 1 (January 7, 2014): 23.

neither one would dream of doing so. Taking it easy, they feel, is for those who can do nothing else: the very young or the very old, the sick and handicapped, and perhaps monks and nuns in their monasteries.

The image of the cowled and hooded monk gazing placidly across a lake, with nothing to do all day but contemplate eternal verities, is pure myth. The cloister walls contain their own variety of workaholic while concealing him or her from the world's view. Contemplative leisure is available in our monasteries, but so is work, and often it is work that prevails. There is always work to be done, and nearly all of it can be justified as a means of self-support or a service to others. The consequence, however, is a spirit of activism in monastic communities.

The monastery may still wish to give a communal witness to the transcendent value of contemplative adoration and liturgical prayer, but in fact it has acquired a reputation for being a model dairy farm, school, bakery, or cheese factory. Industries and work projects that began as small enterprises, little more than one person's hobby, tend to expand, acquire momentum, demand more labor and capital, and absorb more time, until it seems that the community is there to keep all the work projects going instead of the other way round.

Individual monks or nuns can make so large a personal investment of time and interest in a particular project that its success or failure reflects on their own self-esteem. They identify themselves more as professionals in their specialized field of work than as consecrated religious. As they make work the all-encompassing dimension of their life, they become less sensitive to other people's interests, talents, or feelings, less inclined to appreciate the finer details of beauty and culture, less willing to become involved in community activities not related to their work, and less able to spend time with the Lord in sacred reading and contemplative leisure. The workaholic may wear a monastic habit instead of a business suit, but the profile is the same.

Raising Lazarus

What are some of the factors, both conscious and unconscious, underlying the workaholic syndrome? Some therapists say that workaholism is a symptom of deeper personal issues. Workaholism may be a way of coping with underlying emotional problems, anxiety, feelings of inadequacy. What is the workaholic trying to prove or avoid?

Monks and nuns usually have high personal standards, and some of us are perfectionists, in the sense that we cannot simply do our best and leave it at that. We cannot say, "If it's worth doing, it's worth doing badly." We cannot bring ourselves to say, "That's good enough," and walk away. No, it is almost never good enough. Perfectionists tend to be workaholics. Although perfection has been unattainable since the fall of Adam and Eve, perfectionists feel compelled to keep pushing, keep trying harder and going faster. The perfect end product is always a little beyond their grasp, the finish line always out of reach. If that goal should ever be reached, a new one would pop up immediately.

Henri Nouwen has suggested that something about solitude and silence provokes anxiety. He writes, "Many people who say how much they desire silence, rest, quietude would find it nearly impossible to bear the stillness of a monastery. When all the movements around them have stopped, when nobody asks them a question, seeks advice or even offers a helping hand, when there is no music or newspapers, they quite often experience such an inner restlessness that they will grab any opportunity to become involved again."[17]

Our nearest opportunity for staying involved is often our daily work, or a hobby. We plunge into these activities until the feeling of uneasiness is deadened. What is it about silence and solitude that arouses such uncomfortable uneasiness? When we are quiet and alone, with a large block of unstructured time at our disposal, we are vulnerable to feelings of emptiness whose intonations can often be drowned out by activity. Keeping busy, even at trivial

---

[17] Henri Nouwen, *Reaching Out* (Garden City, NY: Doubleday, 1975), 52.

things, postpones the encounter with our self. That confrontation might reveal a poverty, a need for transformation and conversion that we prefer not to admit. Some people never step on a scale for fear it will show they are overweight and should reduce. If we are continually on the go, we will have no time left for ourselves. We can lose ourselves in work. Work gives us something tangible and visible to deal with, something we can control. The successful results of our work give us a satisfying sense of being worthwhile. Work dulls and deadens the hollow emptiness we feel whenever we are alone.

Work can keep us from looking at problematic areas of our life such as interactions with other persons. If communicating and relating to others makes us feel slightly uncomfortable or inadequate, we might be tempted to bury ourselves in some form of impersonal work where we do not have to deal with people so much as with machines or with animals and plants. We may be able to function very peacefully and smoothly as long as we do not have to work with other people. Keeping constantly busy with impersonal work is a way of avoiding clashes and maintaining the illusion that all is well.

Work can shield us not only from ourselves but also from God. The monastery is structured so as to facilitate the search for God, but once God begins to manifest something of his power and nearness, we shrink back in fear. The mystery of God not only draws but also frightens us. The Letter to the Hebrews says our God is "a consuming fire" (Heb 12:29). Work offers us effective insulation when we are not sure how close we want to get to that divine fire. The encounter with God is uncontrollable, and we would feel safer with something tamer. So we turn to legitimate monastic pursuits like making hay, raising tomatoes, molding statues, and fixing rosaries. Commenting on this defensive reaction before an overpowering reality, Annie Dillard quotes Thomas Merton: "Thomas Merton wrote, 'There is always a temptation to diddle around in the contemplative life, making itsy-bitsy statues.' There is always an enormous temptation in all of life to diddle around making itsy-bitsy friends and meals and journeys for itsy-bitsy years on end. . . . The world is wilder than that in all directions, more dangerous and bitter, more extravagant and bright. We are making hay when we should be making whoopee; we are raising tomatoes when we should be raising Cain, or Lazarus."[18]

Making whoopee is for the carefree, and raising Cain is for the indignant; raising Lazarus is for those who have dedicated themselves to living the Paschal Mystery of death and exaltation. Those who refuse to insulate themselves from the consuming fire of God may, like Lazarus, go through a mystical death and rising to new life.

Toward a Balance

The workaholic is a slave to the spirit of doing instead of being, abiding, enjoying. The workaholic finds it difficult to sit still; once movement ceases, sleep becomes irresistible. The hectic pace of the workaholic's life offers apparent proof of importance and indispensability. The life of perpetual activity has been playfully caricatured by Antoine de Saint-Exupéry in *The Little Prince*. The little prince came in his travels to a planet owned by a business-man. "This man was so much occupied that he did not even raise his head at the little prince's arrival."[19] He ignored his visitor in the hope that he would not be distracted from his important work of counting the stars, which he owned and administered. The little prince began to question him, and finally the business-man could ignore him no longer: "Eh? Are you still there? Five hundred-and-one million—I can't stop. I have so much to do! I am concerned with matters of consequence. I don't amuse myself with balderdash. Two and five make seven."

The little prince persisted, and the businessman told him that the last time he had been disturbed in his work was eleven years

---

[18] Annie Dillard, *Pilgrim at Tinker Creek* (New York: Bantam, 1975), 276. The Merton quotation is taken from *Contemplation in a World of Action* (New York: Image, 1973), 354.

[19] Antoine de Saint-Exupéry, *The Little Prince* (New York: Harbrace Paperbound Library, 1971), 52. Subsequent quotations are taken from pp. 52–55.

earlier: "I was disturbed by an attack of rheumatism. I don't get enough exercise. I have no time for loafing." The little prince went on asking questions and the businessman went on trying to count: "There is no time for idle dreaming in my life. . . . Five-hundred-and-one million, six-hundred-twenty-two thousand, seven-hundred-thirty-one. I am concerned with matters of consequence: I am accurate."

Eventually the little prince had to leave, because the businessman would give him none of his time. He had no time for amusement, for exercise, for dreaming, or for relationships with other people. He was little more than a talking, organic calculator. He had lost his humanity through years of continuous absorption in his work. He thought he was concerning himself with "matters of consequence," but the most important and fulfilling activities of life he considered a waste of time. The things that make life worth living can be appreciated only when we slow down and work in a more balanced and human way.

We can avoid the addiction of workaholism if we keep a balance of sacred reading, liturgy, and work. In a balanced day, we set limits to our work time so that work does not dominate and crowd out sacred reading or liturgy. In the weekly cycle we try to keep Sunday as a day of spiritual and physical rest, doing necessary chores only. At the same time, we do not have to be compulsive about keeping the traditional balance. There will be exceptional times when extra work is necessary. In monastic life, generally speaking, doing and making things are not as essential as being, seeing, loving, and worshipping. A good balance is reached when workdays alternate with Sabbaths and involvement alternates with withdrawal.

Work and Rest

"On Sunday," says Saint Benedict, "all are to be engaged in reading except those who have been assigned various duties" (RB 48.22). Other exceptions include brethren who are unwilling or unable to do sacred reading and who would waste their time in idleness; they too are commanded to work on Sunday. Still,

Benedict's principle is that Sunday be a day free of work, a day of rest, the day of the Lord.

The Sabbath rest, of course, is an explicit precept in the Old Testament: "The seventh day is the Sabbath of complete rest, holy to the Lord" (Exod 31:15). So sacred was the Sabbath that working on that day was punishable by death. Slaves, resident aliens, and even beasts of burden were to rest on that day (Exod 20:10). If the Sabbath rest was a duty, it was also a privilege. By keeping the Sabbath, the creature imitated and participated in the repose of the Creator on the seventh day: "He rested on the seventh day from all the work he had undertaken" (Gen 2:2).

The anthropomorphic language of Scripture glides over the fact that work and rest are not mutually exclusive in God, since God's being transcends both; God is his rest and his activity simultaneously. For human beings, to rest from work was a sign of a Godlike freedom and dignity. The Sabbath rest symbolized the liberation of the children of God and their sublime destiny of sharing the very life of God in his kingdom.[20] The Sabbath provided rest for weary human limbs, but its principal purpose was to provide an opportunity for praising and glorifying the Lord, joyfully celebrating him on a day "holy to the Lord" (Exod 31:15).

Jesus added a new dimension of meaning to the Sabbath rest. The Pharisees insisted on abstaining from all forms of work on the Sabbath. Jesus said that as far as external observance goes, "the Sabbath was made for man, not man for the Sabbath" (Mark 2:27). He insisted on abstaining from evil deeds and on doing good, on offering mercy not sacrifice, on an interiorization of the Sabbath (Matt 12:6-7). In Jesus, the Sabbath found fulfillment because he brought true rest to the human heart and true liberation from the yoke of sin. By shouldering the yoke of his cross and "bowing his head" to rest in death (John 19:30), Jesus liberated the world from sin. On the day after the Sabbath, Jesus, the "Lord of the Sabbath," rose in glory (Mark 2:28; 16:1). It was "the Lord's day" (Rev 1:10). The primitive Christian community began the

[20] See Deut 5:14-15 and also Abraham Joshua Heschel, *The Sabbath* (New York: Farrar, Straus and Giroux, 2005).

custom of gathering every week "to break bread" (Acts 20:7) on the day Jesus rose, which was the first day of the Jewish week and the Day of the Sun according to the pagan calendar. After Constantine made Christianity the state religion of the Roman Empire, Sunday became an official day of rest from work.

Celebrating Sunday

Monastic life as a whole has a Sabbath quality in anticipation of that eternal Sabbath when all creation will be free from slavery to corruption, and when God "will wipe every tear from their eyes, and there shall be no more death or mourning, wailing or pain, for the old order has passed away" (Rev 21:4). In our contemporary Western culture, many people reserve one day a week for rest and the worship of God, but monks and nuns consecrate their entire lives to the worship of God. We also work, obviously, but monastic work need not destroy the Sabbath quality of monastic life if the work is done for the glory of God and if the work is prudently balanced with times of leisure, especially on Sundays.

When monastic work is balanced with contemplative leisure, life takes on a daily or weekly rhythm that is in harmony with interior bodily rhythms and the natural rhythms of light and darkness, growth and rest, wind and calm. In monasteries with an agricultural economy, there is also the seasonal rhythm of more to do in summer and less in winter. Even on a farm, Sunday should if possible be a day when people do something different from what they do the rest of the week. It might be a day for developing cultural values or giving time to a creative hobby or going out for a long walk. Then Sunday becomes a time of re-creation from within, a time of breathing in and gathering one's forces in preparation for another week of expending oneself.[21]

---

[21] The healthy alternation between active and contemplative modes of presence is described by Kay Leuschner: "Be active, have dominion, fill the earth, use, make, control: be masculine—that is good. But on the seventh day, make holy, disengage, come back to self, into wholeness; be useless;

Sunday is not merely time for ourselves. Sunday is time for the Lord; it is the Lord's Day. Saint Benedict prolonged the celebration of liturgy on Sunday and expected more time to be spent in sacred reading. When we put aside the cares of our daily work and turn to the Lord, we do so with loving trust in his care for us and for all the aspects of our work. We turn our cares and our work over to the Lord, confident that all will be in good hands and nothing will be lost if we take this one day off. On Sunday we are free. "This is the day the LORD has made; let us rejoice in it and be glad!" (Ps 118:24).

When Sunday is well kept, the Sunday spirit of freedom and celebration can enter into our weekday labors and transform them. Gerhard Martin has suggested "every day should be Sunday." He explains: "'Every day should become Sunday' means that freedom and joy increasingly penetrate to everyday life, that they permeate it like a ferment. The quality of Sunday should enter into everyday life, thus even into the suffering and the toil and labor."[22]

The monk or nun who works with an inner attitude of celebration can bear a witness that the world of today needs to see. We can demonstrate that it is possible to labor without being dehumanized, to take work seriously and yet to work in a relaxed and leisurely way, to work hard without losing a free and playful spirit. Instead of the compulsive, driven attitude of a slave toward work, we have the attitude of those who are free, those who work when it is time for work but know how to relax when the work is over. A Sunday attitude toward weekday work can keep us from becoming too stressed and insistent that everything be done absolutely to a t. Trusting in God's loving care, we simply do the best we can and accept the result for what it is. The Sunday mentality transforms a compulsive worker into a relaxed, gentle, carefree, compassionate human being who realizes that the horizon of life extends far beyond his or her particular work project.

---

worship: be feminine—that is good. Know God." "The Hunger of Eve," *Review for Religious* 36 (January 1977): 83.

[22] Gerhard Marcel Martin, *Fest: The Transformation of Everyday*, trans. Douglas Meeks (Philadelphia: Fortress Press, 1976), 39.

Conclusion

We work for the same reason we do sacred reading and join in liturgical prayer—as a means of truly seeking God. The more our work loses this intention and becomes merely a means of self-support, the less it becomes a monastic practice. Work has its legitimate and necessary place in our daily occupations, but workaholism and hyperactivism give too large a place to work. The present chapter has stressed the need for balancing work with other equally important elements of monastic life. When work alternates with sufficient contemplative leisure, we may learn to work in a prayerful and leisurely fashion. Then our work provides an apostolic benefit for others and restoration for ourselves in body and spirit. When our activity is balanced with Sabbath rest, we already anticipate the eternal Sabbath rest in God, to be spent in spiritual activity that is not exhausting but restful in itself. Monastic life orients us toward that day when God will give us rest in himself. Of that day Saint Augustine wrote, "[It] shall be brought to a close, not by an evening, but by the Lord's day, as an eighth and eternal day, consecrated by the resurrection of Christ, and prefiguring the eternal repose not only of the spirit, but also of the body. There we shall rest and see, see and love, love and praise. This is what shall be in the end without end."[23]

Questions for Reflection

What strategies would you recommend to prevent monastic workaholism?

Does the monastic tradition of manual labor continue to be viable in a high tech society?

---

[23] Augustine, *The City of God* 22.30, trans. Marcus Dods (New York: The Modern Library, 1950), 867. See a similar thought in Augustine's *Confessions* 13, quoted by Samuele Bacchiocchi, *Rest for Modern Man* (Nashville, TN: Southern Publishing Association, 1976), 24.

SENIORUM SAPIENTIA

SIT NOBIS

ET TECTUM

ET

FUNDAMENTA

IV

CUSTOMS

Once when a television personality was being interviewed about the pressured, nerve-jangling world of his profession, he felt obliged to admit that he sometimes envied those who had more pattern and predictability in their lives. He confessed to a recurring fantasy about an artist supposedly living in a remote village of the Southwest who rides a horse to his workshop every morning, makes a turquoise bracelet, then rides back home in time for dinner and goes to bed at the same time every night.

The fantasy of this overactive TV celebrity bears some resemblance to the orderly life in a large monastery. The exterior pattern of community life is determined by the daily schedule that governs predictable, customary behavior from the hour of rising to the final prayer service of the day. Yet if the celebrity were to follow the monastic schedule and customs for a period of time, he might find the structure too confining, even monotonous in its repetition. Customs can chafe and annoy.

Adapting to the customs of the group is one of the first challenges of monastic life. There is a monastic way of doing things, a monastic way of living, that may seem strange at first because the reasons underlying it are not immediately evident. Monastic customs do not always include the quickest, most efficient and economical, or even the most meaningful, way of doing things, and yet they are to be followed. The trend in recent times has been to reduce and simplify customs so they correspond better to local needs while remaining within the limits of broader, general norms.

Living by Custom

Later we shall reflect on particular customs such as common meals or the recitation of the Angelus. But what can we say about the value of customs in general? Our monastic customs or practices, including liturgical rites, enshrine values that have been considered important by those within the tradition. Customs regulating the place and duration of conversation, for example, protect the values of silence, charity, and fraternal support. Other customs have been designed to inculcate a spirit of reverence or humility or self-discipline, such as the custom of greeting others silently.

A custom such as the frequent ringing of bells that was found helpful when first introduced tends to perpetuate itself, even when the connection between the concrete practice and the underlying purpose has been obscured by changing circumstances and mentalities. Newcomers are quick to ask, "Why do we have to do it this way?" If no genuine reason can be given, perhaps the time has come to revise the custom through the accepted community decision-making process.

Sometimes, however, the real reasons are difficult to formulate or do not sound persuasive when formulated. Experience can bring to us meanings that we can appreciate more by living than discussing. The customs in a monastery all have their part in the total process of transformation taking place in monastic life. They invite us to surrender to them, to trust them, to listen for their inmost meaning, to grow with them and be nourished by them for a lifetime. No single one of these customs may be essential to monastic life, but taken together and lived with generosity they help constitute an environment that opens one to the encounter with God.

Customs not only enshrine and communicate monastic values; they are themselves a value. For example, fidelity to the day schedule with its balanced alternation of work, sacred reading, and liturgical prayer will in the course of time mold and shape us into recognizable facsimiles of monks or nuns. Customs teach us to be monks or nuns not only in external behavior but also, on a deeper level, by calming, freeing, and stabilizing our responses and creating a sense of order and security. Because it is repetitive and periodic, customary behavior affects a personality on the preconscious level. Whether I am aware of it or not, my human spirit looks for familiar landmarks and familiar companions on its journey through each new day. If each day were unpredictable from beginning to end, I would soon lose touch with reality and feel bewildered, lost, unanchored, adrift; such is the path to psychosis. When, however, there are familiar landmarks that I can rely on, I develop a feeling of security. I know for example, that I can count on a hot meal being ready for me at a particular time each day, because that is the custom at my monastery. For the community as a whole, these unchanging customs help create a sense of corporate identity. A group defines itself, in part, by its customary behavior.

If you traveled from monastery to monastery throughout the United States and lived in each one for a sufficient length of time, you would see variations in monastic customs. Although most of the customs will be the same because they are inherited from monastic tradition, the way they are observed in each monastery is unique to each place. There are variations adapted to the unique circumstances of each monastery. Another influence is the ethos or spirit of the monastic lineage going back to Europe and transmitted from mother house to daughter house. These are some of the variables you would observe in your visits to Benedictine and Cistercian monasteries. I think your conclusion would be that customs are relative, that there is no one, perfect way of doing things. Different circumstances suggest different solutions.

Monasteries often gather their customs into a booklet called a *Customary* or *The Usages* or *Community Guidelines*. Their purpose is to help newcomers learn all the customs and to help the seniors remember them all. Among the Trappists, a book called *The Usages* was followed for many years throughout the Order.[1] Around the middle of the 1960s, a revised and slightly simplified version appeared in a larger format. At that time, the Trappists were still trying to maintain uniformity of observances worldwide. At the 1967 General Chapter, the concept of uniformity of observances gave way to the dual concept of "unity and pluralism," and the book of usages or customs was reduced to a list of eleven points in a *Statute on Unity and Pluralism*. Individual monasteries were permitted to develop their own customs as long as they were faithful to eleven points. For example, no. 4 said: "The hour of rising is so regulated that vigils, which follows it, should keep its traditional character of nocturnal prayer—as we watch for the coming of the Lord."[2] That was all. There was no mention of the exact time of rising, as found in the previous books of usages. The result was that most monasteries went on rising at the hour to which they were accustomed, about 3:15 a.m. Some monasteries, however, took advantage of their freedom and changed the hour, whether to get up earlier or later, as long as it was still nighttime when they celebrated Vigils, "watching for the coming of the Lord." Some monasteries could be very flexible about adding an hour of sleep whenever the previous day had been unusually strenuous or when sickness was going around. It is an example of treating customs not only with respect but also with a certain degree of freedom. As Jesus reminds us, "The sabbath was made for man, not man for the sabbath" (Mark 2:27).

Customs exist in order to inject some predictability, along with some degree of flexibility, into a person's life, so that when one

---

[1] For a commentary on this book, see Thomas Merton, *Monastic Observances: Initiation into the Tradition*, ed. Patrick F. O'Connor, MW 25 (Collegeville, MN: Cistercian Publications, 2010).

[2] General Chapter of Abbots, *Statute on Unity and Pluralism*, 1967, http://www.ocso.org/index.php?option=com_docman&Itemid=126&lang=en.

wakes up in the morning he or she has some sense of what to do and when to do it. Others in the community will be doing the same things at the same time. Predictable customs strengthen togetherness in the community. Custom assures the community of an ordered style of living that fosters contemplative deepening. The pervading good order creates an atmosphere of stability and serenity within which the individual can be free to concentrate on prayer. When there is a dependable order, people begin to feel at home in the monastery, in the world, and in life as a whole. That feeling of at-homeness is fertile ground for the word of God to take root and grow. Recall the parable of the sower; it was the seed falling on good soil that took root, grew, and bore abundant fruit (Matt 13:8).

Resistance

Newcomers to monastic life usually have plenty of good will and want to fit in and do what is expected of them. They may, however, already be formed in their own customary ways of doing things, for example, sleeping late. A change of behavior seems almost impossible, even with good will. Some of the community customs feel like a straitjacket to them. Furthermore, the monastic way of doing things can seem counterintuitive, just the opposite of what one might do spontaneously. Why should I close doors quietly in the monastery when I can slam a door behind me to make sure it is closed? Monastic customs are not always the quickest way of doing things, nor is it always easy to see a deeper spiritual meaning in the custom. So the newcomer is tempted to start a new custom in order to show the seniors a better way.

Instead, the newcomer could be encouraged to give the monastic customs a try, conform to them, and see if they become more meaningful with the passage of time. There are things that we can appreciate only by long experience of them. Customs are meant to surround us gently and comfortably from the time we rise in the morning until the time we retire. Spiritual deepening usually takes place in the simple, unruffled flow of everyday living. It is custom that assures a smooth flow throughout the day. When we accept the rhythm of customary behavior and begin to flow with it, we experience the power it has to quiet the surface level of life so that we can be more aware of the spiritual goal and purpose underlying all that we do.

Repetition as Life-Giving

The structure of life in a monastic community is like the structure of a well-designed building, except that the design is in behavior instead of steel or stone. Design implies an organizational unity with a variety of parts in balanced harmony. Repetitive or customary behavior creates design in the community and in the life of each individual in the community. There is a certain internal pressure toward conformity to customs, just as there is a cohesive force binding the parts of a building together. Observing accepted community customs gives an individual a sense of belonging to the group. To live according to the customs is felt to be right, while deviating from the customary behavior seems wrong, because it breaks the conventional pattern that binds the community together.

Although spiritual deepening does not usually occur in a climate of chaos and unpredictability, still, "where the Spirit of the Lord is, there is freedom" (2 Cor 3:17). An overstructured way of life stifles the spirit. Instead of meaningful customs, there are meaningless repetitions, lifeless ceremonies, lockstep processions, compulsive acts performed under pain of neurotic guilt feelings. Such rigidity rightly arouses negative reactions. Communal customs do imply repetitive behavior, but in a monastery such repetition exists for the sake of affirming the religious, aesthetic, or social values of the community. Often the value is simply that of stable, good order. Community customs may be observed faithfully without precluding a playfulness and flexibility that permit occasional deviations. We can respect and observe our community customs without making idols of them.

Resistance to customary or ritual behavior may come from a passion for newness that is common in our culture today. Many expect something different every time. They have a low tolerance for "the same old thing." Anthropologist Margaret Mead has commented, "We don't want to read the same book twice or to see the same play over again or to be betrayed into viewing again the same program on television."[3]

Contemporary, mass-media culture thrives on variety. Monastic culture, in contrast, is based on fidelity to the same familiar customs. The community of the present is linked to its own past and to the heritage of monasticism by the frequent repetition of customary monastic practices. The community's vision of monastic life is fostered by the members' shared experience of customs that return again and again. How can such repetitive behavior be preserved from meaninglessness and boredom? Sometimes a deliberate personal effort may be necessary. If I do not like doing things this way, I may have to search deliberately for deeper motives and for deeper levels of meaning in this custom. I may have to invest some emotional energy in what I am doing and try to love this particular activity for the sake of loving monastic life as a whole.

Customs are sometimes resisted because they are perceived as a threat to one's natural, spontaneous behavior. I may feel that getting up at 3:15 a.m. is not my style. The early hour does not suit my spirituality or fulfill my personal growth requirements. For me this custom is counterproductive. Yet the community's schedule calls for rising at 3:15 a.m., and if I sleep in every morning I will feel less a part of this community. The dilemma suggested by this example is the perennial problem of balancing one's need to be oneself with one's need to be a member of a group. Can both needs be satisfied?

A monastery is a community of the followers of Christ where his Paschal Mystery is celebrated and proclaimed in power. By

---

[3] Margaret Mead, "Celebration: A Human Need," in *Twentieth Century Faith: Hope and Survival* (New York: Harper and Row, 1972), 126, as quoted in Lucille Meissen, "Worshipful Living: Attitudes for Spirituality," unpublished master's thesis, Center for the Study of Spirituality, Duquesne University, Pittsburgh, 1977, 45.

dying we rise to new life; by losing ourselves we find ourselves in the mystery of Christ. In my adjustment to community customs I experience this truth. It is when I give myself to the community and to the customs of the community that I possess myself as a free person. When I forget myself, I rise to a new consciousness of self. When I let go of my own familiar habits and customs, the customs of the community can communicate to me their life-giving power. By participating fully and ungrudgingly in community rituals and customs, I emerge as a more complete and resonant expression of the unique individual that I am. Then it will be obvious to me that customary monastic behavior is the way monks and nuns act spontaneously.

Monastic life is not a body of customs and rituals any more than Christianity is a code of church laws. Following the customs of the house will help one blend into the community, but it would be an illusion to think a person becomes a monk or a nun merely by knowing and observing all the customs. The monastic vocation is realized interiorly and exteriorly when a person freely expresses his or her own unique personality by living according to the customs of the community.

Change of Customs

A loving respect for traditional customs seems to be part of the monastic spirit. Monks and nuns are generally not quick to leave tried and tested ways for ways that are novel and risky, however full of promise. Innovators are likely to be suspected of lacking humility because they give the impression of thinking that what was good enough for the seniors and sanctifying for them is no longer good enough.

It takes humility to accept and adapt to new customs, because I am accepting other people's ways of doing things, not my way, not my will. Humility says, "not my will but yours be done." Saint Benedict recognizes that the effort to adapt is a sign of advanced humility. He writes, "The eighth step of humility is that a monk does only what is endorsed by the common rule [that is, the customs] of the monastery and the example set by his superiors"

(RB 7.55). Where no written code determines practice, follow the example of the seniors. Ideally the seniors should all be doing the same thing, the same way, the monastic way. This ideal, however, is not always realized in monasteries, and a newcomer may be led astray by imitating the bad habits of a particular senior. The senior to imitate is one who knows and keeps the rules.

If monastic life is truly alive, however, there will be growth and evolution. A community that never changes is a dead community. Customs need to be evaluated from time to time. An example of evaluation long overdue is described by author Cleveland Amory in a scene at the breakfast table of the distinguished and proper eighteenth-century federal judge, John Lowell of Boston. All was proceeding according to custom until a maid came in to whisper a message in Mrs. Lowell's ear. The judge's wife hesitated a moment and then broke the bad news to her husband. There is no oatmeal this morning. A reaction of disappointment if not outrage might have been expected, because Judge John Lowell had been accustomed to having oatmeal at breakfast for almost his whole life. But the judge merely lowered the newspaper he had been scanning and said to his wife, "Frankly, my dear, I never did care for it."[4]

In a well-managed abbey, the oatmeal is less likely to run out, and any effort to alter long-standing customs may be perceived as threatening the peaceful order of community life to which the majority of members has grown accustomed. Those introducing changes in monasteries have a difficult task, although it may be their vocation to raise a prophetic voice within the community and to plant the seeds of new ideas whose time will come. The initial response to their efforts, however, is likely to be discouraging. They should expect to encounter resistance from those who cannot envision the benefits of any other set of customs and will not feel at home if the changes are extensive or rapid.

Suppose there is a custom that you consider to be obsolete or senseless. First, recognize that what is making that judgment may

[4] Anecdote from https://bible.org/illustration/oatmeal, citing *Bits & Pieces* (March 4, 1993): 23.

be your ego, your prideful self, the part of you that always wants to look poised. Ego feels like saying, "Go ahead, guys, do it your way. Don't wait for me. I'm going to sit this one out, because it doesn't make any sense to me." Monastic humility, in contrast, says, "It looks dumb, but I am going to give this practice a try anyway." As Jesus promised, "Whoever loses his life for my sake and that of the gospel will save it" (Mark 8:35). When I lose or let go of my own judgments, preferences, familiar habits, then the customs of the community can communicate to me their life-giving power. Then I find life; I save and preserve my life. Where is life for a cenobitic monk or nun? It is where my brothers or sisters are right now, doing what they are doing. When all are chanting, working, sleeping, or eating, that is probably what I should be doing also, patiently and generously participating in the common customs and practices.

The common ways are to be given a fair trial, and their hidden meaning and wisdom given time to emerge. Only when it is obvious, first to a prophetic individual and then to many others, that the common ways have lost their helpfulness would a change of custom be indicated. The necessary adjustments will then be accepted without widespread loss of peace or a lasting polarization in the community. Changes are inevitable and even desirable, but the rate and manner of the changes are to be monitored prudently for the good of all.

Particular Customs

Some monastic customs and rituals are associated with particular occasions such as Christmas or Easter and the seasons of the liturgical year. Other customs are associated with the daily Eucharist and Divine Office. Then there are liturgical rituals that we observe occasionally: processions through the cloister, profession rites and burial rites, the last three days of Holy Week culminating in the Easter Vigil service with its powerful use of natural symbolism. Here, however, I will comment on several customs that we encounter daily within the life of a monastic community.

The Angelus

Three times a day the bell tolls and I interrupt whatever I have been doing, turn toward the church or the tabernacle, and silently recite the Angelus. The words of this prayer repeat the dialogue of the annunciation scene: God's invitation to Mary through the angel and Mary's response. The Angelus, which developed in stages beginning at least in the thirteenth century, is more than a manifestation of monastic devotion to Mary. It is possible to discern a connection between the Angelus and the central goals of monastic life. The annunciation scene recalls the mystery of God's respect for our freedom to accept or refuse his continual gift of grace. God will not enter my life or my heart without my free consent. The Angelus is a daily opportunity, presented in a ritual way, for me to consent to God's gift of himself to me, and to say, "Here I am, Lord . . . I am ready." Repeating Mary's words of acceptance becomes my act of yielding to God's will for me in the present situation. Day after day this custom places me before God in an attitude of total personal surrender, reaffirming my monastic commitment.

Examination of Conscience

Many monasteries schedule one or two periods a day for personal examination of conscience, usually in the context of the Divine Office. William of Saint Thierry (d. 1148) advised the brethren to examine their consciences every day and "stand before God to see the reasons for joy and sorrow in their actions, and to feel true remorse for their sins."[5] The *examen* is a moment of review, repentance, and recentering, and the practice is not restricted to monks and nuns. In a book meant to help overworked businessmen alter their lifestyle and so avoid heart attacks, we read, "Each day at noon, try to find yourself. . . . Use your lunch

[5] William of St. Thierry, *The Golden Epistle: A Letter to the Brethren at Mont Dieu* 1.29, trans. Theodore Berkeley, CF 12 (Spencer, MA: Cistercian Publications, 1971), 48–49, quoted by Janet Burton and Julie Kerr, *The Cistercians in the Middle Ages* (Woodbridge, Suffolk, UK: Boydell, 2011), 84.

period as an opportunity to meet yourself. Until you try seriously to discover what is the *essence* of your life, and find out how to disengage it from the garbage of the days and years, your life will not be graced by peace—or your heart (most literally) with tranquility."[6] A period of examination makes good sense even on the purely human level of meeting myself, getting in touch with my feelings and longings, reviewing the direction my life is going. Adding a faith dimension to the practice, I can use the period of *examen* to place this day before the Lord and renew my intention to trust more totally in his love and his guidance.

Concretely, my *examen* might include the following steps:

- I begin with a moment of grateful remembrance of God's gifts to me this day and ask for divine help now to make this *examen* fruitful;

- I quickly replay the day to see whether my words and activities have been born out of a sense of God's presence and as a response to the call of love in each situation;

- honestly, but without depression or shame, I ask God for mercy and healing, confident that God loves me in spite of my frailty and brokenness;

- finally, I commit myself and the rest of my life to God as his faithful servant for the future.

Such an exercise need take only a few minutes, but if it seems too elaborate, the first two steps can easily be omitted.[7]

Community Meals

The custom of having at least one meal a day in common expresses and fosters a sense of community. Ideally, everyone should be present, although in practice this is often impossible. The dining

---

[6] Myer Friedman and Ray H. Roseman, *Type-A Behavior and Your Heart* (New York: Alfred A. Knopf, 1974), 214.

[7] The daily *examen* is highly recommended by Ignatius Loyola in his *Spiritual Exercises*. He suggests five steps. See http://www.jesuit.org /spirituality?PAGE=DTN-20130520125910.

room itself should be an inviting place in which to gather for a shared meal, a place kept neat and clean and attractive, a place suited for the importance of the occasion. "The structure of our life together," says Sister Maria Goretti Blank, "should provide for uninterrupted time to eat leisurely, in a calm and relaxed manner. This atmosphere is significant for more than the biological benefits of proper digestion and the enjoyment of our food."[8] A monastic dining room is not simply a place to eat, a fast food restaurant where someone can fill up and run. Our eating habits may have been influenced by the contemporary filling-station approach to meals. Our culture pays the price in gastrointestinal difficulties and in the loss of the ability to enjoy the simple pleasure of taking food together in fellowship and mutual respect.

In contrast to the filling-station approach, where having to eat is the only reason for coming to the dining room, the community might foster a more celebratory approach. We gather as a family and celebrate our common life by sharing food, just as we celebrate our common faith by breaking bread together during Mass. In fact, a text from the sayings of the Desert Fathers associates these two tables: "One of the Fathers used to say that three things are important for monks, to which they should be attached with fear and trembling and with spiritual joy: communion in the holy mysteries, the common table, and washing the feet of the brethren."[9] The dining room table becomes an extension of the Lord's Table, because at both we partake of a meal that expresses our oneness and affirms the presence of God as the center of that oneness.

The Rule prescribes reading rather than conversation during meals (RB 38.5). The gathering of the community in the dining room is a sign of oneness and shared life. Exclusion from the common table is a form of excommunication: "If a brother is found guilty of less serious faults, he will not be allowed to share

[8] Maria Goretti Blank, "On the Relationship of Embodiment to Spiritual Unfolding," unpublished master's thesis, Center for the Study of Spirituality, Duquesne University, Pittsburgh, 1976, 2:1023.

[9] *The Wisdom of the Desert Fathers: The Anonymous Series*, trans. Benedicta Ward (Oxford: Fairacres, 1975), no. 239, p. 64.

the common table. . . . He will take his meals alone, after the brothers have eaten" (RB 24.3, 5). The reading that Saint Benedict prescribes is one of the elements that bind the group together; this oneness can be felt when the reader comes to a humorous passage and everyone spontaneously laughs at the same time.

Determining the measure of food and drink, Saint Benedict selected a simple, frugal standard that would prevent gluttony and drunkenness (RB 40.1-9). The practice of fasting and abstinence will be discussed in chapter 8. Here we note that Benedict's norm not only safeguards waistlines but also fosters a sensitivity toward food. Eating leisurely and in silence, I may rediscover the language of food itself. There is a mysterious osmosis, a mutual honoring, taking place between me and the food I consume. Something of planet Earth is being used to sustain me and is being elevated and transformed as I consume it.[10]

Listening to the language of the food will help me transcend a merely physical, functional mode of eating. The portions on my plate, arranged in a colorful collage that appeals to sight, smell, and taste, speak of more than physical nourishment. The food before me represents, collects, gathers, and draws in the sun, earth, sky, rain, the grower, producer, handlers, the cook—implicitly the whole interconnected world.[11]

The experience of eating involves not only taking food but also giving myself to the activity of taking food. I put aside the concerns of work for this half hour in the day and give myself to an interval of rest and refreshment. I take time to enjoy the meal and to enjoy also the companionship of those with whom I sit at the table, even in silence. The community meal is a venerable monastic custom. In our day, it may be worthwhile to reflect on the meaning of the common table in order creatively to tap its potential as shared life and as a means of deepening that life.

---

[10] See Bernard de La Héraudière, "The Monastic Meal," trans. Abbey of Our Lady of the Prairies, *Monastic Exchange* 8, no. 1 (Spring 1976): 72–74; no. 2 (Summer 1976): 29–32.

[11] This thought is from an unpublished talk by Dr. William Kraft, given on July 1, 1977, at Wellsburg, West Virginia.

Dishwashing

When the community meal has been finished in peace and good fellowship, can we prolong that cooperative spirit during the dishwashing after meals? Customs vary about who washes the dishes and how the task is done, but dishwashing is one of those necessary chores that almost everyone in the community is expected to share.

Saint Benedict may have included dishwashing among the chores of those who were assigned to kitchen service each week. According to chapter 35 of the Rule, the only exemptions from this service were those who were already engaged in some important task for the community. Exemptions from disagreeable duties tend to multiply. People are quite willing to enjoy eating what is put on their plate but not always willing to wash the plate afterward. During meals we can find satisfaction and perhaps even a sense of the sacred, but the dishwashing might seem devoid of religious meaning. As we roll up our sleeves for this work, we shift into the gear of pure functionality and might not expect to find religious value in the dirty dishwater. Could that be a mistake? The dualistic notions we tend to have concerning what is sacred and what is profane are mercilessly laid bare in a story about the Zen master who said to a disciple seeking instructions for enlightenment, "Have you eaten? . . . Then wash your bowl. If you cannot find the ultimate justification of existence in an act as simple as that of doing the dishes, you will find it nowhere."[12]

At Madonna House in Ontario, a training center for the lay apostolate, the guests and staff are all expected to join in the dishwashing after the principal meal. One guest was a woman who had come for a visit in order to learn about Christian community. The topic of community had been the subject of lofty and inspired discussion during the meal, and the new guest showed an inclination to prolong the heady conversation afterward. Then

[12] Huston Smith, *The Religions of Man* (New York: Perennial Library, 1965), 151.

someone suggested that she might experience Christian community for herself if she would join the dishwashers.

During the meal, God can be found in the sharing of a common table; after the meal, God can be found in the lowly experience of dishwashing. The monastic ideal of holistic living—*monos* in the sense of whole, integral—runs counter to any dualist current of spirituality that tends to separate spiritual from corporal activities. The custom of daily dishwashing can help promote a monastic spirituality that seeks and finds God in everything.

Daily Eucharist

In Egyptian monasticism, and probably also in Saint Benedict's time, there were eucharistic celebrations only on Sundays and feast days. With the multiplication of priests in the Middle Ages and beyond, daily Mass grew more common until eventually it became the general practice in monastic communities. In our time, the pendulum may be swinging back, as some monasteries, especially of nuns, experience a scarcity of priests and chaplains. As long as it is possible to celebrate the Eucharist daily, it will continue to be a spiritually significant custom in its very dailiness.

There the dailiness of my entire monastic life finds meaning, because there the mystery of Christ is made present. There I draw the strength needed to face the tasks and difficulties, sometimes the pain and suffering, of everyday life, and to face the routineness of that life. Just as my body benefits from daily physical nourishment, so my spirit benefits from daily contact with the living bread of this sacrament. Furthermore, the faith and love that it takes for me to recognize the Lord in the breaking of the bread at Mass are precisely the attitudes I need in order to recognize him also when I meet him, disguised, in daily life. If I can recognize him in the eucharistic bread and wine, perhaps I shall also recognize his presence hidden in the bread and wine of daily events, daily encounters with my brothers or sisters, daily work, sacred reading, and prayer.

On the material level, there can be too much of a good thing, but not on the spiritual level. In one of her published letters, the Southern Catholic author Flannery O'Connor said that she would never be able to explain, except in a story, why she felt the Eucharist was such a central reality. She was challenged once at a small gathering of intellectuals who agreed that the Eucharist was a good symbol but no more than that. Flannery O'Connor responded with a remark that may have shocked her sophisticated friends: "Well, if it's a symbol, to hell with it." For her, the Eucharist was far more: "It is the center of existence for me; all the rest of life is expendable."[13]

Conclusion

Monastic customs bring order and design into life. We have seen that customs change slowly, and that there is good reason for this gradual approach. The traditional customs enshrine values that can be fully appreciated only by lived experience and conscious reflection. Customs are a monastery's bond with other monasteries of the same family and with the entire tradition of monasticism. Particular customs, however, can challenge us to discover the word of life they still communicate. Subsequent chapters will take up this challenge as we consider many other monastic practices, both individual and communal.

Questions for Reflection

How would you go about introducing into your monastery or home a custom from a different culture?

If a custom having to do with food or drink becomes expensive, should it be discontinued as contrary to poverty?

---

[13] Sally Fitzgerald, ed., *The Habit of Being: Letters of Flannery O'Connor* (New York: Farrar, Straus and Giroux, 1979), 125.

obsculta et vide et inclina aurem tuam :

concupiscet rex decorem tuum

MONASTIC COURTESY

Monastic courtesy or decorum has to do with the personal manner according to which people conduct themselves appropriately in any situation. Courtesy may be considered part of the customs of a particular monastery. Courtesy brings a quality of graciousness and propriety to everything we say or do. Of itself, courtesy is not a proof of sanctity or purity of heart, because external behavior may be insincere. When it is sincere, courtesy may be considered the spontaneous expression of an interior harmony, the exterior reverberation of an inner gracefulness and dignity. When we are being ourselves, our graced selves, we will radiate a certain charm, attractiveness, and kindness both in speech and deeds, and we will have an instinctive feeling for the right thing at the right time. Monastic courtesy flows from the heart outward, manifesting the intense but gentle love at life's source. It is one of the delicate forms of love.

Monastic courtesy includes not only politeness, civility, etiquette, and good manners but also a good manner. Our personal manner or style is part of our innate uniqueness shaped by family background as well as formation in the monastic school of the Lord's service. There is a difference between what we do and how we do it, between simply doing the correct thing and doing it in a way that is pleasing and attractive to others. Decorum makes our goodness beautiful in the sight of others. "So will the king desire your beauty [Vulg: *decorem*]," says the psalmist (Ps 45:12). A pleasing manner is the fruit of a long, favorable life experience and shows itself in an instinctive consideration for the feelings of others and a spontaneous preference for good form and the proper social amenities.[1]

The scriptural context for monastic courtesy is found in the example of Jesus, who was "meek and humble of heart" (Matt 11:29), and in the general New Testament stress on love and peace toward all, even toward enemies (Matt 5:44). Poured out in our hearts by the Holy Spirit, love is the shared life of respectful fellowship in the monastery. Saint Paul's famous chapter on love in his First Letter to the Corinthians is a charter for monastic courtesy or decorum: love is patient, kind, not snobbish, never rude or self-seeking, not prone to anger (1 Cor 13). When he wrote to the Ephesians, Paul exhorted them to "live a life worthy of the calling you have received, with perfect humility, meekness and patience, bearing with one another lovingly" (Eph 4:1-2).

Saint Paul's idea of the external relations of Christians presupposed courteous decorum. He expects us to show respect to everyone because everyone is the image of God and is my brother or sister in the extended family of God. A monastery should reflect the family of God, an all-inclusive family in which all deserve respect as fellow human beings who have been loved into being by God our Father and redeemed by the blood of Jesus our brother to be a dwelling for their holy and life-giving Spirit.

---

[1] Courtesy goes beyond good manners and is more difficult to teach, but even the teaching of good manners is so neglected that it becomes newsworthy when a school hires a full-time teacher of manners. See *Saturday Review* (March 1, 1980): 6.

Some Historical Perspectives

Saint Benedict devotes chapter 63 of his *Rule* to the theme of preserving good order in the monastery by doing things according to seniority. Seniors are to be shown due respect. He bases his thought on a text from Saint Paul that encourages Christians to respect one another: "Anticipate one another in showing honor" (Rom 12:10). Other contemporary translations of the New Testament bring out the meaning more clearly: "Have a profound respect for one another" (Jerusalem Bible); "Be eager to show respect for one another" (Good News for Modern Man). From this principle, Saint Benedict drew practical conclusions about monastic courtesy governing the respectful titles by which the monks were to address one another or their abbot and governing the protocol when monks met one another in the cloister. It could have been a common occurrence that two monks came to a doorway at the same time; the *Rule* and the virtue of courtesy directed the junior to defer to the senior, letting him go ahead after first requesting his blessing (RB 63.15-16). One's standing in community gatherings was not determined by age or class but by time of entry into monastic life or by special decision of the abbot. Juniors were to honor their seniors and the seniors to love their juniors. Seniority provided Saint Benedict with a simple principle for the orderly movement and interaction of large numbers of people.

In the sixteenth century, the English author Edmund Spenser wrote *The Fairie Queene,* a lengthy allegorical poem about the virtues. The Knight Calidore in Book 6 is the knight who represents courtesy. Describing courtesy as a humanizing and civilizing quality, the poet asks,

> What virtue is so fitting for a knight,
> Or for a Lady, whom knight should love,
> As Courtesy, to bear themselves aright,
> To all of each degree, as doth behove?[2]

---

[2] Edmund Spencer, *The Fairie Queene*, bk. 6, Canto 2, http://www.sacred-texts.com/neu/eng/fq/fq67.htm.

British author C. S. Lewis, in his commentary on *The Faerie Queene*, describes courtesy as "the poetry of conduct." Just as not everyone can write poetry but only those who have this gift, so there are people who seem to be courteous by nature. They do not study it or assiduously practice it but have it as a grace of life because they are full of genuine love toward their neighbor and are humble in themselves. Lewis says that someone with this virtue of courtesy will be "immediately loveable to all who meet him." He concludes by saying that courtesy is "the bloom (as Aristotle would say)—the supervenient perfection—on the virtues of charity and humility." It is an added luster on the basic Christian and monastic virtues of love and humility.[3]

Thus a monastery is expected to be a place where the monks or nuns are courteous to one another because they are full of charity and humility. Anyone who meets such a monk or nun will smile with joy to encounter someone "immediately loveable to all who meet him." Was not Jesus such a person? The bruised reed he did not crush (Isa 42:3) because he came not to crush life but to restore it. Often in the gospel we sense the deep courteousness of our Savior. Some of the Fathers of the Church, both Latin and Greek, liked to speak of the divine "condescension" that led God to accommodate himself to human beings and come down to our level in the mystery of the incarnation. Thus God is our model of courtesy.

We note that *courteous* contains the word *court*, suggesting a royal court and the proper manners or decorum expected in the presence of royalty. The fourteenth-century romance *Sir Gawain and the Green Knight* depicts the courtesy of a well-bred knight of King Arthur's court, Sir Gawain. In the Middle Ages, among the troubadours and love-singers, a favorite theme was courtly love and chivalry. It was the age of chivalry or, what amounts to the same thing, courtesy, the art of not giving offense. Courtesy implied that a person knew the appropriate, noble way of acting, especially as regards relations between the sexes. One of the uncanonized saints who was swept away by the thought of

[3] C. S. Lewis, *Allegory of Love: A Study in Medieval Tradition* (Oxford: Oxford University Press, 1958), 351–52.

the courtesy of God was Julian of Norwich (1342–1416). She was an anchoress, meaning that she lived in a cell called an "anchorhold," built against the wall of a church in Norwich, Norfolk, England. In May 1373, Julian received a series of powerful supernatural visions that she meditated on throughout the remainder of her life, calling them *Revelations*. They led her deeply into the gospel truth that God is love and that God delights to make his dwelling in the hearts of his faithful. The theme of God's *courteous* love is pivotal in her understanding of the gospel, although she uses the term only nine times.

Julian talks about God's "marvelous courtesy that comes from his abundance of love." God shows a kind of hospitality to humans: "Then our courteous Lord shows himself to the soul cheerfully with glad countenance, with a friendly welcome." Julian talks about the courtesy of Jesus, giving us himself in the Eucharist: "The mother may give her child to suck her milk, but our precious Mother Jesus, he may feed us with himself, and does full courteously and full tenderly with the blessed sacrament of his body and blood that is precious food of very life. And with all the sweet sacraments he sustains us well mercifully and graciously."[4]

Personal Decorum

Decorum looks in two directions: toward self and toward others. Loving self-respect and loving respect of others determine the propriety of our speech or behavior. First, we have to ask whether a particular mode of behavior is compatible with our own dignity and self-respect and with our growth toward holiness and human wholeness. Second, we need to ask how this behavior will affect others. These are the questions that determine courtesy on the personal level and on the interpersonal level. The present section takes up personal courtesy.

---

[4] Julian of Norwich, *Showings*, trans. Edmund Colledge and James Walsh (New York: Paulist Press, 1978). Julian's word *courtesy* is derived from the French word for *court* and probably denotes a courtly manner, with connotations of noble, generous, benevolent, considerate, and respectful dealings.

Neatness and Cleanliness. Despite exceptional vocations like that of Saint Benedict Joseph Labre, dirtiness is not a sure sign of holiness. Cultural customs have evolved beyond those that led Saint Benedict to say, "the healthy, and especially the young, should receive permission [for baths] less readily" (RB 36.8). Today, frequent and even daily showers are to be recommended, particularly after strenuous work. Elementary requirements of personal hygiene cannot be neglected. If they do not go to extremes, monks and nuns are rightly concerned about their good physical appearance. Their concern extends also to their garments and shoes. With care, the monastic habit can be kept respectably clean between washings. The cowl deserves special care and even respect, for it is the outward sign of monastic consecration.[5] Neatness and cleanliness should be evident also in one's private cell. Living in dust and dirt is unhealthy as well as unedifying. A cluttered room and desk might be the sign of a cluttered heart.

Words and Actions. Monastic courtesy remembers such basic points of etiquette as polite table manners and the appropriate use of "please" and "thank you." A gentle person will use a gentle touch in dealing with things, rather than a heavy-handed, abusive touch that destroys things and leaves a shambles in its wake. Ours should be the touch of one who uses things respectfully and gratefully, not grasping them and clinging possessively to them but touching them lightly and then letting go. We can learn to move through life sedately and with dignity, not perpetually on the run, two or three steps at a time. There are occasions when haste is necessary, but the galloping-goose type of person is perpetually in a hurry. In Saint Benedict's teaching, the twelfth degree of humility is to carry oneself with bowed head and lowered gaze as an exterior sign of a recollected heart (RB

[5] Some have seen symbolism in the cowl's shape that suggests the angelic winged figures of Isaiah's heavenly vision (Isa 6:2) and also the cross that the monk or nun must take up daily in imitation of the Master (Luke 9:23). Since the cowl is without opening in front or back, it may symbolize a final commitment. Saint Benedict did not want his disciples to be overly concerned about the color or quality of their clothing, as long as the fit was satisfactory and the thickness adequate for warmth (see RB 55).

7.63). Restless, wandering eyes betray an interior restlessness. According to Saint Bernard of Clairvaux, the first step of pride is the spirit of curiosity manifest when a person cannot control his or her desire to see who comes in, who walks by, where he is going, what he is eating, reading, or wearing. Bernard drew an amusing sketch of a curious monk: "Wherever he is, standing, walking or sitting, his eyes are wandering. His glance darts right and left, his ears are cocked. . . . These symptoms show his soul has caught some disease. He used to watch over his own conduct; now all his watchfulness is for others."[6]

Courtesy and the Anima. Many contemporary psychologists hold that each person carries within himself or herself both masculine and feminine elements, called by Carl Jung *animus* and *anima*.[7] Ancient Taoist teaching expressed a similar distinction by the terms *yin* and *yang*. Men identify with their masculine side, the *animus*, but still carry within them an unconscious feminine side; for women the reverse is true. A sense of propriety and courtesy seems to be largely a function of the *anima* or the feminine within.

Perhaps personal courtesy comes more easily in houses of nuns than of men, but it is not something of concern only to women. Courtesy is something that men need to cultivate also, because it is an expression of love. In all monasteries, courtesy can be fostered by showing appreciation for one another's creative efforts to bring harmony and beauty into the surroundings. Appreciating people's efforts encourages them to take responsibility for the small details of daily life in common. Inappropriate or disturbing behavior calls for a tactful, disapproving response. Outbursts of pettiness need not be reinforced by showing tolerant amusement. Charity and civility require the conscious effort always to be gentle but firm when making corrections.

---

[6] Bernard of Clairvaux, *The Steps of Humility and Pride*, trans. Ambrose Conway, in Bernard of Clairvaux, *Treatises II*, CS 13 (Spencer, MA: Cistercian Publications, 1974), 57.

[7] See M. C. D'Arcy, "Animus and Anima," chap. 7 in *The Mind and Heart of Love* (New York: Henry Holt, 1957), 174–93.

Men who live for a long time in solitude and silence or in exclusively masculine company tend to neglect social amenities and grow careless about courtesy. Some revert to primitive, boorish standards of conduct, and expect their rude, uncouth behavior to be acceptable to others. Flatulence, belching, halitosis, and body odor may be tolerated in military barracks, prison cellblocks, or nursing homes, but such disrespect toward others is offensive in monasteries. Offensive also is language spiced with vulgarisms, off-color stories, or profanity. "No obscenity or silly or suggestive talk, which is out of place," cautions Saint Paul (Eph 5:4; cf. 4:29). Sometimes a certain roughness in speech and behavior is intended to be a sign of masculinity, but this is a false masculinity. Gentlemanly decorum does not diminish true masculinity but adds luster to it. What is diminished by decorum is only the false manliness of machismo, the coarse, he-man swagger that is unsure of its own manliness.

Monastic courtesy allows for the influence of the *anima*. To the *anima* belong appreciation of beauty, intuition and insight, a quality of delicacy, sensitivity to little things, a knack for soothing troubled relationships, a power of creativity and inspiration, of authoring and nurturing life, a feeling of being at home in the world, a healing and comforting touch, a natural gracefulness of movement. Especially important in monastic courtesy is the *anima's* care for harmonious interpersonal relationships, for putting people at ease and making life comfortable for them.

Part of the normal human maturation process for both men and women is to come to terms with the *anima*, accepting its tendencies as a healthy part of oneself, valuing and serving its orientations. If someone denies the *anima*, these same potentialities will turn against him or her. Repressed *anima* does not die and disappear; it manifests itself in warped and twisted forms. If the *anima*, the gentle woman within, is not recognized, she gets her own back by turning into a moody, nagging, crabby, unruly, insufferable witch. If the *anima* has not been accepted and integrated by old age, the result is likely to be an old man or woman with a crotchety, miserly, angry, or rude personality instead of a wise, good humored, respectable senior who is a treasure in the community.

Courtesy in Community

Courtesy looks toward others and asks what effect this behavior of mine will have on others with whom I live. Will it disturb them? Will it interrupt the silence and solitude to which they have a right? Will it cause them pain in any way? Or embarrassment? Monastic courtesy is a basic expression of fraternal charity. When courtesy prevails, the monastery will enjoy peaceful, friction-free living.

Courtesy, based on charity, was the legacy Saint Benedict desired to leave his communities when he came to the concluding chapters of his Rule. In his description of the good zeal that his disciples ought to foster, he stresses first their courteous conduct toward each other: *"They should each try to be the first to show respect to the other* [Rom 12:10], supporting with the greatest patience one another's weaknesses of body or behavior" (RB 72.4-5).

Monastic courtesy in the concrete prescribes leaving things the way I myself would like to find them: cars with fuel in them or butter dishes with butter on them. When I finish a work project I should clean up the debris and put the tools away in good condition. Cleaning up after myself includes cleaning things like the dishes, shower, or sink I have used. I am aware that someone else will have to use it after me. If I spill something, it is I who should clean it up, either immediately if it is going to be in someone's way, or at a more convenient later moment. If I have used the last of something, it is I who should replace, refill, reorder it, or notify the one in charge so that there will be something there when the next person comes for it. It takes only a little extra time to replace an item that is in common use. The next person will never know I did it and never thank me for it, but he or she will be inconvenienced if I fail to take the time to do it.

The person who has no time to bother about such things may be pursuing only what is good for himself or herself. Monastic courtesy means taking time, even for little things. Things that affect other people are important, but people themselves are more important. Courtesy implies taking time for people, for being sociable and listening to them, for anticipating their needs, for commiserating with their problems and pains in a respectful, nonintrusive way. Gentlemanly or ladylike courtesy is not prone to press one's own opinions, philosophies, or politics, one's own taste in music, art, literature, or spirituality, on one's brothers or sisters. Instead of lecturing them on our way of doing things, we prefer gently to let them be and become fully themselves in an environment of warmth, respect, and fraternal love.

Blessed John Henry Newman once wrote, "It is almost a definition of a gentleman to say that he is one who never inflicts pain."[8] Like a good host or hostess, the courteous person's great concern is to make others feel at ease and at home and to spare them pain. When people live closely together, they are certain to bump against each other and even injure one another unless each exercises a gentle sense of decorum and courtesy. By being sensitive to others, we can often ease an uncomfortable situation and preserve our neighbor's dignity. Courtesy helps to oil the gears that are supposed to mesh smoothly in our communal interactions; otherwise there will be too much friction and annoyance with one another. The social philosopher José Ortega y Gasset has observed that courtesy flourishes in countries where people live closely together, the only other alternative being communal self-destruction. He writes,

> Courtesy . . . is a social technique that eases the collision and strife and friction that sociality is. Around each individual it creates a series of tiny buffers that lessen the other's bump against us and ours against the other. The best proof that this is so lies in the fact that courtesy was able to attain its most perfect, richest and most refined forms in countries whose population density was very great. Hence it reached its maximum where that is highest, namely, in the Far East, in China and Japan, where men have to live too close to one another, almost on top of one another. Without all those little buffers, living together would be impossible. It is well known that the

---

[8]John Henry Newman, *The Idea of a University*, Discourse 8, http://grammar.about.com/od/classicessays/a/A-Definition-Of-A-Gentleman-By-John-Henry-Newman.htm.

European in China produces the impression of a rude, crass, and thoroughly ill-educated being.[9]

Aelred of Rievaulx (1110–1167) was abbot of a Cistercian monastery of some six hundred monks in Yorkshire, England. How did he hold the place together? The Holy Spirit was undoubtedly helping him do it, but undoubtedly also most of those six hundred monks had to be practicing the virtue of civility (that is, courtesy, decorum) toward one another, in order to survive as a community. Aelred wrote a still-popular treatise on *Spiritual Friendship*.[10] He was teaching his six hundred monks to live together as friends.

Conclusion

The deepest root of monastic decorum is respectful, courteous love of oneself and of one's brothers or sisters. Such love is the gift of the Holy Spirit, who dwells in our hearts and in our midst. Catholic historian Hillaire Belloc (1870–1953), in a poem called "Courtesy," sensed "that the grace of God is in courtesy."[11] As we have seen, the English mystic Julian of Norwich loved to dwell

---

[9] José Ortega y Gasset, *Man and People*, trans. Willard Trask (New York: W. W. Norton, 1963), 168. Ortega's reference to the Orient may be illustrated by one of the sayings of Confucius: "Tsekung asked, 'Is there one single word that can serve as a principle of conduct for life?' Confucius replied, 'Perhaps the word *reciprocity* will do. Do not do unto others what you do not want others to do unto you'" (Lin Yutang, *The Wisdom of China and India* [New York: Random House, 1942], 831).

Confucianism, the principal ethic of China for two thousand years, also stressed the principle of *Li* or ceremonial. *Li* governed every situation: "To begin with, ceremonial (*Li*) provides the means for the regulated handling of special occasions, such as birth and death, in a man's life. Next ceremonial provides an implement as well as a yardstick of propriety in human conduct. Finally, ceremonial provides an element of adornment and grace, so that a man's life may achieve some degree of balance and beauty" (*Encyclopaedia Britannica*, 15th ed. [1975], *Macropaedia*, 4:1094).

[10] Aelred of Rievaulx, *Spiritual Friendship*, ed. Marsha L. Dutton, trans. Lawrence C. Braceland, CF 5 (Collegeville, MN: Cistercian Publications, 2010).

[11] Hillaire Belloc, *Sonnets and Verse* (New York: Sheed and Ward, 1944), 57.

on the courtesy of God. She writes, "The greatest abundance of joy which we shall have, as I see it, is this wonderful courtesy and familiarity of our Father, who is our Creator, in our Lord Jesus Christ, who is our brother and our savior."[12] Human courtesy and decorum may be seen as a participation in the "wonderful courtesy" of the triune God himself. By the grace of God, our loving courtesy enables us to see a reflection of the divine goodness present in all realities, events, and persons, including ourselves. Sometimes we will have to look deep beneath the surface, but love gives us a power of vision that perceives our neighbor's underlying godliness, affirms it, and fosters its full emergence into the light of Christ. In the Sermon on the Mount, Jesus asks us to "be perfect, just as your heavenly Father is perfect" (Matt 5:48). Just as our heavenly Father's love is courteous toward us, our love for one another needs to be courteous and sensitive. Monastic courtesy helps everyone live monastic life with joy, so that in the monastery, as Julian of Norwich says, "all manner of things shall be well."[13]

Questions for Reflection

Why should I continue to show courtesy to someone who always disrespects me?

Because of their upbringing, some people have little appreciation for courtesy. Is it too late to educate them in this value? How might I attempt it?

---

[12] Julian, *Showings*, chap. 7.
[13] Julian, *Showings*, chap. 27.

your word, o lord, came down

SILENCE

One of the most characteristic monastic practices, one stressed from the origins of monasticism, is silence. The difficulty that many experience with prolonged silence was once illustrated by a cartoon showing a novice in his monastic cell apparently engaged in animated conversation with a ventriloquist's dummy on his knee. In the adjacent room a monk comments, "Brother seems to be having a problem with the rule of silence." Meant to facilitate conversation with God, monastic silence drives some to talk to themselves.

In the monastery, silence is a deliberate practice, a discipline that we willingly take up. People outside the monastery may not know very much about monastic life, but typically they believe that monks, especially Trappists, take a vow of silence. They think we are called "Trappists" because we keep our trap shut! Often we have to explain to visitors that Trappists never have taken a vow of silence, but we do practice silence in the monastery for the sake of devout reflection.

A life of prayer and recollection in a communal context requires some degree of genuine silence. If monks and nuns are responsibly prudent about keeping quiet at certain times and places in the monastery, ample opportunities remain at other times for openness and sharing. Silence balances speaking in a prayerful, sociable monastic community. Both silence and conversation have a common root in the spirit of attentive listening.

While all members of a community may agree on the importance of silence, some would prefer less and others more. House customs should respect individual differences and the special needs or legitimate inclinations of each monk or nun. Not everyone is immediately capable of prospering in silence. Newcomers to monastic life may need more communication until they have learned ways of using silence profitably. They may be introduced to the silent life gradually but seriously. They will never learn to love silence unless they make an effort to be silent instead of communicating every thought that comes into their head and commenting on everything they notice or hear about. One learns to be silent by being silent, rather than by talking about silence or reading about it or listening to conferences on it.[1] It is more important to enter into silence and let silence enter into you until it feels natural to you.

Nature is predominantly silent, except for the sounds of insects, birds, and animals, which do not really destroy the underlying silence of nature. Silence is the ambiance that nature chooses, so that life may flourish, may evolve. The big bang at the beginning of creation must have been a silent bang, because there is no sound in the vacuum of space. Silence is prior to sound; it is the milieu from which sound emerges and to which it returns.

---

[1] Nevertheless there are significant, present-day studies of silence from various points of view. See the following: Maggie Ross, *Silence: A User's Guide*, vol. 1, *Process* (Eugene, OR: Wipf and Stock, 2014); Bonnie Thurston and David Steindl-Rast, *Practicing Silence: New and Selected Verses* (Brewster, MA: Paraclete Press, 2014); Newsletter "Friends of Silence," http://friends ofsilence.net/page/welcome-friends-silence; Documentary "In the Pursuit of Silence," http://www.pursuitofsilence.com/trailer-no-1/.

Biblical Backdrop

The Bible tells us that it was in the wilderness of the Sinai desert that Israel learned to depend on God as on her covenant partner. The desert is a silent place. In the silent desert Israel listened to the word of God and not to the idols. After reaching the Promised Land, however, Israel paid heed to the seductive voice of idols. The prophet Hosea predicted that, once again, God would renew in the silent desert the covenant that Israel broke: "I will allure her now; I will lead her into the wilderness and speak persuasively to her" (Hos 2:16). The imagery is of a bridegroom wooing his beloved back to him, alluring her, speaking to her heart. For us, God uses the silence of the monastery to allure us to himself and speak words of love and mercy to our heart.

In the gospels we find Jesus, who is the very Word of God, saying nothing in public until he was about thirty; he was content to live a hidden life for all those years. Except for one episode in the temple when he was twelve, not a single word of his has been preserved from that period. This is not to imply that he was mute. Instead, it was as if Jesus was incubating his mission in silence until the appointed hour came for that mission to emerge. During his public ministry he related favorably to silent people, like the woman with a hemorrhage who silently crept up behind him and silently touched his cloak (Mark 5:27). Jesus himself sought silence and solitude for prayer, even at night. He refused to say a word in his own defense during his trial, silent as a sheep before its shearer (Matt 26:23; 27:12; Isa 53:7).

Jesus was the prophetic word of God, even in his silence. Those who share in his prophetic mission, as monks and nuns do, cannot neglect silence. Before he can proclaim the word of God, the prophet must hear the word, and only the silent hear. Because of our silent life, we may be in a better position than anyone today to read the signs of the times and hear what the Spirit is saying to the Church. All of us have the vocation to hear that word of God in silence and to bear witness to it by the fidelity of our lives. Some of us may have the added prophetic mission of proclaiming to the world the word that it needs to hear. Only the purity of our prophetic silence guarantees that we are proclaiming the word of the Lord and not the echo of our own interior noise. Silence has always been the milieu in which the word of God has been heard most clearly and understood most completely.

Ambiguity of Silence

The practice of silence has its risks because silence is not always a value. There is an unhealthy and negative silence, a silence of death. Noncommunication can express mute rebellion, obstinate refusal, deep resentment. By not speaking, one can often avoid being challenged, avoid taking a stand, avoid the relationship that may become too involving, avoid the demands of love. A marriage can be ruined when one partner decides to punish the other by giving him or her the "silent treatment." Silence may be a sign of an underdeveloped personality, an introspective, suspicious, moody, morose type of character. Or silence may indicate a vacuum of indifference and be the sign of a haughty, aloof disinterestedness. Such silence is a closure, a selfish shut-ting-the-world-off, a withdrawal behind closed doors posted with a "Do Not Disturb" sign.

Silence becomes virtuous when it is practiced out of love for God and for others. Silence creates a climate that facilitates recollection and conserves the fruits of recollection. Instead of being a form of closure, the silence of the monastery should express an openness to others and hospitality to the world. This silence is oriented to sustaining life. A love of silence is characteristic of the monastic spirit.[2] Our silence is born of an attentiveness that

---

[2] William of St. Thierry relates his impressions on visiting the abbey of Clairvaux for the first time around 1143, emphasizing the observance of silence: "Entering the clear valley from over the ridge, the very first glance visitors got sufficed for them to *recognize God in the abbey's buildings* [Ps 47:4]. In the simplicity of construction and the humility of those dwellings, the mute valley itself bespoke the simplicity and humility of the *poorfolk of Christ* [EC 2.7] who dwelt within them. Then too, in that valley, so full of people, no one was allowed to be *idle* [RB 48.1]; all were toiling, each at the task assigned. Yet new arrivals would nevertheless meet in full daylight a silence characteristic of the dead of night: no sound but that of the toil or of

puts us at the disposal of the word that will be spoken to our heart (see Hos 2:16). Even if the word is spoken softly, it falls like a fertile seed into the receptive soil of our silence. The word is retained by silence and given a home where it can accomplish its work of transformation.

The continual pouring out of words can leave our spirit depleted and dissipated. Silence restores us to ourselves. Silent persons are self-possessed persons who hold themselves in readiness either to speak or to hear. They are available to the word. The silent monk or nun welcomes, gathers, and takes to heart the words of distress, the cries of pain, the pleas for help that rise from the suffering world. We in turn present these cries to God in intercessory prayer, holding the world in our heart before the Lord. Visitors often experience our silence as an invitation to vent their personal needs or fears, to request the prayers of the community, or to share with them their joys and gratefulness.

Practice of Silence

In his chapter on the practice of silence, Saint Benedict quotes the Latin version of Psalm 38:2-3: "I said I have resolved to keep watch over my ways that I may not sin with my tongue. I was silent and was humbled, and I refrained even from good words" (RB 6.1).[3] Benedict concludes that his disciples should refrain not only from sinful speech but "even from good words" out of esteem for silence. Silence is the general rule; speech is the exception when a genuine need arises. The first characteristic that Saint Benedict looks for in a candidate to monastic life is that he

---

the divine praise the brethren were engaged in at the moment. Moreover, the observance of this silence, and the prestige it enjoyed, used to instill into newly arrived seculars such a reverence that they were ashamed to utter there, not merely what was improper or idle, but anything beside the point" (William of St. Thierry, "Life of Bernard of Clairvaux," *Vita Prima* 1.1.7; trans. Martinus Cawley, 1.35:246A [Lafayette, OR: Guadalupe Translations, 2000], 35).

[3] *The Rule of St. Benedict 1980*, ed. Timothy Fry (Collegeville, MN: Liturgical Press, 1981), 191.

or she is someone who "truly seeks God" (RB 58.7), someone truly absorbed in the quest for the living God, someone intent on the one thing necessary (see Luke 10:42). By the grace of their vocation, monks and nuns lean more toward being quiet than toward speaking, although by nature and temperament they might not be so inclined. Some monks and nuns are introverts by temperament and have a natural bent toward quiet. Those who are extroverts have a natural bent toward expressiveness, but grace helps them to live the silent life without doing violence to their temperament.

Because we are committed to maintaining a prayerful and recollected atmosphere in the monastery, there are guidelines about when and where to speak. The guidelines require the cooperation of all in order to be effective. The guidelines governing silence in Trappist monasteries have changed over the years. When I entered the monastery in 1960, communication was mostly by sign language and written notes, customs inherited from the seventeenth-century reform at La Trappe. Trappist sign language, similar to the sign language used among deaf people, was deliberately limited in what it could express. Some of the monks were creative and could make up new signs or put signs together with great facility in a sign-conversation; they might just as well have been speaking, except that usually they were not making any noise.

Like Saint Benedict, monks and nuns of our day recognize that silence is a value, but we do not make it the highest value. We can be inclined to silence but at the same time feel free to speak when helpfulness, compassion, and charity indicate that speech is appropriate. If your house catches fire, day or night, do not keep monastic silence. Yell "Fire!" to warn the others.

Love of silence should manifest itself concretely. The level of physical noise in buildings can be reduced by such little things as walking softly, closing doors quietly instead of slamming them, conversing quietly so as not to disturb others, installing silent light switches or putting carpet on stairways, and soundproofing certain rooms. Extra efforts at maintaining silence are called for during the annual retreat, the monthly day of recollection, the weekly desert-day, and the great silence of the night.

Because of our desire to be friendly toward people we meet, we may think we are obliged to say something every time we encounter someone in the monastery. It seems polite to say "Hello" or "How's it going?" In the context of monastic life, however, silence is not impolite. We learn to feel comfortable in the presence of others without speaking to them. In life outside the monastery, silence may seem embarrassing, except among total strangers riding the same elevator, bus, or plane. In ordinary social encounters, a silent pause indicates that someone is a poor conversationalist. Monks and nuns, however, are expected to be lovers of silence, and it is quite acceptable to say nothing when we meet one another, provided we acknowledge the other's existence by a smile or a nod of the head or little wave of the hand. We can meet each other without stopping to chat, and we can work side by side in silence without being at all uncharitable. Silence needs no apology in the monastic life.

Dimensions of Silence

We have been discussing exterior silence for the most part. The practice of exterior silence, difficult enough in itself, is a step toward the more difficult task of bringing the whole self to that inner stillness where we may encounter the One who dwells in silence. "Be still and know that I am God" (Ps 46:11). Inner silence is transforming. One reason people are not comfortable with silence is a fear of what might happen to them in that silence. Henri Nouwen once described solitude as "the furnace of transformation."[4] All the turbulence and noise within us has to be brought to silence and rest, as we move deeper into the experience of the silence of God. As the following three sections explain, silence should gradually pervade first the bodily dimension of our self, then the personal dimension, and finally our human spirit. Monastic life can be experienced as a progressive immersion into silence.

---

[4] Henri J. M. Nouwen, *The Way of the Heart: Desert Spirituality and Contemporary Ministry* (New York: HarperCollins, 1981), 25.

The Vital Life.[5] Silence in the vital or bodily dimension of the self involves stilling those drives that may deaden my sensitivity to the word and the silence of God, such as the desire for intense pleasure and sensual satisfaction. Also it is helpful to learn personal ways of relaxing tense nerves and muscles. Hatha Yoga exercises may help certain people toward this bodily stillness. We should be able to sit still without compulsive fidgeting or falling asleep. Bodily silence also implies that during community gatherings we try to moderate our noisiness—coughing, sneezing, blowing the nose, belching, clearing the throat, and heavy breathing. Singing and whistling, even when alone, may have to be toned down or completely avoided so as not to disturb others.

The Personal Life. At the personal level of the self, ego raises an inner clamor by its aggressive and ambitious drives, its tendency to manage, control, and organize all of life for its own glory. Ego, selfishness, is the source of noisy disturbance, first in our heart and then outwardly. Ego moves us to seek positions of power, to surpass others in our achievements, to collect an assortment of security blankets, to insist on our rights and reputation. We will experience rest and stillness on this level only when we learn to let things be and to trust that our life is guided by a higher wisdom that invites us to surrender to its mysterious but loving ways.

Our relationships with others in the community originate in the personal dimension of the self. Silence in this area means a right use of speech. We need to silence the word that wounds and cuts down another in his or her presence and the word that judges or ridicules another in his or her absence. We can also practice the silence of listening patiently and openly, with full attention, as another speaks, letting him or her finish speaking before we respond. The monastic ideal is not to become a mute, unfeeling figure like a stone statue. In a later chapter, on community and communication, we will see that our silence has to be balanced with wholesome fraternal communication. Learning that balance is a delicate art, but we will never learn it unless we

---

[5] On silencing the body, the ego, and the human spirit, see Adrian van Kaam, *The Dynamics of Spiritual Self-Direction* (Denville, NJ: Dimension Books, 1976), 509–13.

can learn to control our tongue. Silence is not as important as love, but ideally it is an expression of love.

The Spirit. The most difficult dimension of the self to bring to silence is the spirit—the part of us that believes, hopes, and loves, that rejoices in beauty and appreciates freedom, that opens out to the totality of all that is, that understands, intuits, loves. Our human spirit is created to follow the Holy Spirit of God until it rests in God forever, but our spirit also has the power to raise itself in prideful opposition to God. The spirit of pride and ambition has to surrender silently to God and begin listening to the mystery of God's living silence.

When we silence ourselves on the spirit level, we are at peace and at home in the presence of the Lord of our life. We have quieted the chattering of imagination and memory in order to hold ourselves open to the Holy. We perceive a new richness and beauty in the everyday world about us. In silence, we are content to absorb and appreciate all that happens without commenting on it. We listen more intently to the mystery of nature, letting aesthetic experience direct us toward the silent emptiness where God dwells in the depths of our heart.

Silence opens a way to the depths within. Silence seems to develop its own momentum, drawing us deeper into our true self. At the center of the self there is silence. Ordinarily we do not enter those depths because we feel not in control there; too much silence frightens us. Yet the silence within opens out into the immense silence of God. In order to commune with God we may have to pass through the silence within us.

Hindu monasticism has the practice of making a vow of temporary or even lifetime silence. Such a monk, called a *mouni*, does not even speak interiorly to a particular concept or image of God. Instead the *mouni* stands before the transcendent mystery of God in perfect silence, and his silence is his prayer. The Hebrew prophet Jeremiah said, "Ah, Lord GOD! . . . I do not know how to speak" (Jer 1:6). Then Jeremiah became a spokesman for the Lord God because God placed words in his mouth. The Hindu *mouni* likewise does not know how to speak to God but, unlike Jeremiah, chooses to remain completely silent in the presence of the unspeakable divine mystery.

God can be pictured, though inadequately, as wrapped in silence. Out of silence God spoke a single Word through which the world was created and redeemed; then the Word returned to the silence from which it came. In a Christmas sermon, a twelfth-century abbot, Guerric of Igny, said he wanted to put his ear close "to the secret utterances and sacred meaning of this divine silence, learning in silence in the school of the Word."[6] The silent person lives in readiness to commune with the divine silence.

Silence can facilitate other forms of communication even on the human level. For example, think of two people in love, looking respectfully into one another's eyes, saying nothing yet communicating perfectly.[7] As the silence of the monastery pervades the body, ego, and spirit, a person grows ready to communicate with the silent God on a level deeper than words. Monastic silence in its fullest reality is not simply the absence of noise but the presence of a reality too great for expression. The monk or nun senses in the silence a mysterious depth, substance, density, richness, presence. We are not afraid to let our deep self be invaded by this silence that is the silence of God. We let ourselves rest in that gentle, all-embracing silence of God.[8]

A Carthusian Example

The Carthusians at La Grande Chartreuse in the French Alps allowed themselves to be filmed for a lengthy documentary called

---

[6] Guerric of Igny, "The Fifth Sermon for Christmas no. 2," in *Liturgical Sermons: Volume One*, trans. Monks of Mount Saint Bernard Abbey (Spencer, MA: Cistercian Publications, 1970), 64.

[7] In a letter of July 17, 1901, Charles de Foucauld wrote from the silence of the Trappist abbey of Notre-Dame des Neiges, "Silence, you know, is just the opposite to coldness and forgetfulness; *in meditatione exardescet ignis*. It is in silence that we love most ardently; noise and words often put out the inner fire" (Charles de Foucauld, *Inner Search: Letters 1889–1916* [Maryknoll, NY: Orbis Books, 1979], 84).

[8] See the example of the woman who sat silently knitting before the face of God, as told by Anthony Bloom, *Beginning to Pray* (New York: Paulist Deus Books, 1970), 60–61.

Into Great Silence (2001). Included is a moving interview with an elderly monk who is blind. We also hear the chanting of the Latin liturgy and the sound of the monastery's bells. A brother talks to his cats as he feeds them. Apart from that, there are only the sounds of nature: birds chirping, water dripping, leaves rustling, brooks babbling. Some viewers do not know what to make of a lengthy film with a minimum of speech. They get up and walk out. Some stay to the end, mesmerized by the visual beauty and strangeness of the scenery.

The Carthusians consider silence to be a more adequate response to the transcendence of God than words, even words sung in praise of God. God's incarnate Word was spoken out of silence and can be heard in silence and responded to by silence. The silence is not empty; it is a silence full of love. These silent monks are clearly happy; the blind monk is happy even in his blindness. They do not seem to be troubled about anything, not their future, their health, their next meal, or their neighbor in the next cell. The silence has absorbed all their worries so that they can live in the present moment, focused as much as possible on seeking God. When the film ends, viewers sometimes hesitate to clap, wondering whether it is appropriate to disrupt the silence.

What is appropriate is to *enter* the living silence of *Into Great Silence*, not merely observe it from the outside and admire it. It is holy. It is sacred silence, divine silence. Sacred silence is what makes a life of prayer, a spiritual life, really possible. Someone has said, "All interiority involves a deep relationship to silence."[9] The Rhineland mystic Meister Eckhart perceived a zone of silence at the center of the soul. He says concerning the location of this central silence, "It is in the purest thing that the soul is capable of, in the noblest part, the ground."[10]

Monks and nuns are called to discover and to dwell in this deep and sacred silence. We will not be alone there. "Be still and

---

[9] Therese Schroeder-Sheker, introduction to Robert Sardello, *Silence: The Mystery of Wholeness* (Benson, NC: Goldenstone Press, 2006), xxi.

[10] *The Complete Mystical Works of Meister Eckhart*, 3rd ed., trans. Maurice O'C Walshe (New York: Crossroad Publishing, 2010), flyleaf.

know that I am God" (Ps 46:11). There is another presence with us in the silence. In the stillness, we recall the words of Jesus, "I am not alone, because the Father is with me" (John 16:32). The unseen, silent presence of an amiable companion consoles us. It is the presence of the Consoler, the Paraclete, whom Jesus promised to send, who will abide with us forever.

Conclusion

The practice of keeping silent has been handed down by monastic tradition as an effective means of preparing monks and nuns for the experience of the living God. Although interpersonal sharing through conversation also has a value for charity and therefore for union with God, nevertheless monastic communities need a respectful, loving silence in order to facilitate an atmosphere of meditation.

As we mature in monastic life we grow accustomed to silence, feel more comfortable with silence, come genuinely to love silence. The silence around us in the monastery becomes a silence within us, and the silence within meets and merges with the silence of God. Our inner silence prepares us to hear and receive the silent God. How do we know we are in touch with the silence of God? What does God do in the silence? Often God does not do or say anything. God is simply there, in the mysterious fullness of love. We are aware of an undefinable presence in the silence, and this awareness is a typical form of Christian contemplation. Silence teaches us to pray by holding ourselves quietly attentive and receptive in the divine presence, standing still before God.

Questions for Reflection

Since the Letter of James says "no human being can tame the tongue" (Jas 3:8), is it not futile and unnatural to expect monks and nuns to keep a strict rule of silence?

If keeping silence comes naturally to those with an introverted temperament, what is the most appropriate practice for those who are extroverts?

eructavit cor meum verbum bonum

dico ego opera mea regi

SHORT PRAYERS

Simply to stand in silence before the face of God can be a form of prayer. Unless prolonged by a special grace, however, this stance becomes difficult to hold very long. Like a restless monkey the imagination soon begins its chatter. Our silence is broken, our prayer spoiled.

The Desert Fathers and Mothers aspired to continual prayer, the continual remembrance of God, uninterrupted union with God. They desired to be like Moses on the mountain with his hands continually stretched out in prayer, adoring God and interceding for his people. They wanted to love God as steadily as the human heart beats or as the lungs expand and contract, without a pause day or night.

Saint Paul exhorts all Christians to continual prayer. To the Thessalonians he writes, "Pray without ceasing" (1 Thess 5:17). Monks and nuns have seen in this verse a description of their own goal and ideal. They have given up everything for the freedom to live in heartfelt prayer and loving service. All their monastic customs—liturgical offices, sacred reading, and work—aim at

the purity of heart that makes possible the remembrance of God
in ceaseless prayer. One method that has been found fruitful is
the use of short prayers, also called aspirations.[1]

Short Prayers through the Centuries

We can find examples of short prayers in the Bible, although
without the name. The Old Testament contains liturgical refrains
that make ideal short prayers, such as *Alleluia, Amen*, and the refrain from Psalm 136, "for his mercy endures forever." The book
of Psalms is a treasury of brief, heartfelt prayers.

In the New Testament, the gospel of Luke in particular is full
of such prayers: the plea of the ten lepers ("Jesus, Master! Have
pity on us!"—17:13), the cry of the blind man of Jericho ("Son
of David, have pity on me!"—18:39), the request of the Good
Thief ("Jesus, remember me when you come into your kingdom"—23:42), the prayer of the tax collector ("O God, be merciful
to me a sinner"—18:13), Stephen's prayer as he was stoned to
death ("Lord Jesus, receive my spirit"—7:59). The Lord's Prayer
itself may have been a series of short, rhythmic phrases subse-
quently compiled into the single prayer that has come down
to us in two versions. We know that early Christians also used
exclamations like *Maranatha* ("Come, our Lord," 1 Cor 16:22).

After the New Testament era, some fervent Christians were
still asking how they might be able to pray without ceasing. The
third-century theologian and exegete, Origen, gave one answer.
He understood prayer in a broad sense as a life of love for God
and neighbor. He considered good deeds to be a form of prayer.
According to Origen, a person who lived virtuously and obeyed
the commandments of God in his or her daily occupations and

---

[1] Augustine called short prayers "ejaculations," *orationes iaculatas*, prayers-
shot-like-an-arrow. In a letter to Proba he writes, "It is said that the brothers
in Egypt have certain prayers which they recite often, but they are very brief,
and are, so to speak, darted forth rapidly like arrows, so that the alert attention, which is necessary in prayer, does not fade and grow heavy through
long, drawn-out periods" (*Letters* 130, trans. Wilfrid Parsons [New York:
Fathers of the Church, 1953], 391).

who paused three times a day for explicit prayer was living a life of love in the constant presence of God and could be said to pray without ceasing.[2]

Origen's solution did not entirely satisfy the Egyptian Desert Fathers and Mothers of the third and fourth centuries. They wanted to increase the periods of explicit prayer. By the sixth century, there were seven liturgical Offices during the day and one at night. Eventually they also found a way to bridge the intervals between these Offices by encouraging the private use of short prayers. Short prayers were the preferred means to ceaseless prayer. Monks and nuns could repeat the formula of their short prayer as they worked or ate or even as they entertained visitors.

An illustration is found in the sayings of the fathers and mothers of the desert, traditionally called the *Apophthegmata*. Among these many sayings, we read this anecdote:

> One day we went to visit the old men and as was customary once we had said the prayers and they had greeted us, we sat down. After talking with them we wanted to leave, and we asked them to say a prayer. One of the old men said, "What do you mean? Have you not been praying?" We said, "Abba, there was the prayer when we came, but up till now we have been talking." The old man said, "Forgive me, brothers, but there is a brother sitting with you and talking who has said three hundred prayers." When he had said that, they said the prayer, and took leave of us.[3]

John Cassian (360–435), together with his companion Germanus, visited the monks and nuns who lived in Egypt and questioned them about their style of life. Cassian learned that they used a formula handed down to them "by a few of the oldest fathers

---

[2] "Treatise on Prayer" 12.2, in *Origen*, trans. Rowan A. Greer, The Classics of Western Spirituality Series (New York: Paulist Press, 1979), 104.
[3] *The Wisdom of the Desert Fathers: The Anonymous Series*, trans. Benedicta Ward (Oxford: Fairacres, 1975), no. 148, p. 41.

who were left."[4] The prayer consisted of the opening verse of Psalm 70: "God, come to my assistance! Lord, make haste to help me!"[5] Cassian, or Abba Isaac, whom he was quoting, went on to explain at length that this prayer is appropriate to every situation in life and that it can lead to the highest degree of contemplation.

Through Cassian this formula was transmitted from Egypt to the West. Saint Benedict directed that this verse be used as the introductory verse at the four shorter liturgical Offices. In the first lines of his Prologue, Benedict spoke of praying "most earnestly" to beg God's help in bringing every good work to completion (RB Prol.4). Psalm 70:2 would be ideal for such earnest prayer, although he does not specify it in this place. Later, Benedict does specify that the weekly kitchen server say Psalm 70:2 before beginning his duties (RB 35.17).

Other Traditions

Although Cassian's Abba Isaac, as we have seen, spoke of his favorite short prayer as a tradition handed on by word of mouth, the practice might well have occurred spontaneously even without a tradition because of a natural inclination to remember and dwell on short, meaningful phrases. The use of short prayers seems to be a cross-cultural phenomenon. In the Hindu and Buddhist traditions they are called *mantras*.[6]

Speaking about his own Hindu tradition, Swami Shri Purohit has described the *mantra* used by some of the yogis of India: "They repeat 'Soham' as they draw in the breath and 'Hamsah' as they breathe it out. 'Soham Hamsah' means, 'I am the Hamsa'—the eternal self, or soul.'"[7] In Buddhism, the Pure Land

---

[4] John Cassian, *Conferences* 10.2, trans. Boniface Ramsey, Ancient Christian Writers no. 57 (Mahwah, NJ: Paulist Press, 1997), 379.

[5] Ps 70:2, translation as found in RB 17.3, *The Rule of St. Benedict 1980*, ed. Timothy Fry (Collegeville, MN: Liturgical Press, 1981), 213.

[6] *Mantra* is derived from Sanskrit and denotes a sacred sound, word, or phrase that may or may not have a literal meaning. See the web site Wikipedia, http://en.wikipedia.org/wiki/Mantra#Definition.

[7] Alan W. Watts, *The Way of Zen* (New York: Mentor Books, 1957), 76, 129, 167.

School uses a formula that repeats the name of Amida, a personal divinity, the Buddha of Boundless Light. This formula, called the *Nembutsu*, is seven syllables long (*Namu Amida Butsu*) and means "Adoration to Amida."[8]

Muslims repeat short prayers, the ninety-nine beautiful names of Allah, using a string of beads or a knotted cord that they rapidly pass through their fingers. This practice, which may also use short verses from the Koran, is called *zikr Allah*, the remembrance of Allah. Muslim Sufi brotherhoods adopt a particular prayer formula for group *zikr Allah*, such as "praise be to God," "Allah is the greatest," "I ask God's forgiveness." The repetition, accompanied by proper posture and breathing, crowds everything else out of one's heart until the remembrance of God is firmly established in the Sufi's innermost being. At this point, "the whole being of the Sufi becomes a tongue uttering the *zikr*."[9]

Drawing on the wisdom of both Sufism and Hinduism, Sikhism practices constant repetition of the name of God (*Nammaraga*) to still the wandering mind, cleanse the soul of sin, and open it to the divine light.[10]

As of 2014 more than six million people throughout the world repeat a *mantra* for twenty minutes twice a day in Transcendental Meditation.[11] A Sanskrit word is specifically selected for the individual by an instructor and kept confidential. Repeating this *mantra* quiets the mind and reduces mental fatigue by the vibratory effect of its thought-sound.[12]

---

[8] As found in W. B. Yeats, *Essays and Introductions* (New York: Macmillan, 1961), 430, n. 3.

[9] *Encyclopaedia Britannica*, 15th ed. (1975), *Micropaedia*, 3:513.

[10] *Encyclopaedia Britannica*, *Micropaedia*, 16:746.

[11] Web site of Maharishi University of Management, http://mscs.mum.edu/transcendental-meditation.html.

[12] Harold H. Bloomfield, Michael Peter Cain, Dennis T. Jaffe, and Robert B. Kory, *TM: Discovering Inner Energy and Overcoming Stress* (New York: Delacorte, 1975), reviewed in *Mainliner* (January 1976): 12–20. According to the instructors, there is no connotative meaning in the *mantra*; it is a meaningless word. Reports from private, unpublished sources, however, say that one mantra is *Ram*, the name of a Hindu deity; another is *kilil*, meaning "Kali

Christian Short Prayers Today

In modern Christian devotional practices, the use of repetitive formulas occurs in Centering Prayer, a method that borrows some of the technique of Transcendental Meditation but is based directly on the anonymous fourteenth-century treatise, *The Cloud of Unknowing*. Originating at St. Joseph's Abbey, Spencer, Massachusetts, and now taught systematically at St. Benedict's Abbey, Snowmass, Colorado, and elsewhere, Centering Prayer leads to a simple form of interior silence and union with God in the center of the self.[13] Gentle repetition of a word of one or two syllables, such as "Abba," "Jesus," or "love," sums up the meditator's intention to pray and serves as a vehicle to carry him or her to silent centeredness on God present in the heart. When the word falls away of itself, the meditator lets it go and remains lovingly present to the Lord or waits confidently for the Lord in silence without thoughts. When distractions come, the prayer word can help the meditator to center again on God's presence. The prayer word that is chosen is considered to be a word of life, a word that is life-giving when taken down into the heart and allowed to nourish the roots of faith, hope, and love. Centering Prayer leads to a more centered life.

Another option for prayer based on repetition of a prayer word is Christian Meditation, as developed and taught by two Benedictines, Dom John Main (d. 1982) and his successor Dom Laurence Freeman. Both of these English Benedictine monks went to Montreal and successfully taught this method of Christian Meditation to so many people from all over the world that now there is a well-organized World Community for Christian Meditation. According to the Christian Meditation web site, "In the teaching of the desert monks on pure prayer John Main found

---

should be worshipped for cessation of sorrow." Another *mantra* is Shinim, meaning "Dev should be worshipped."

[13] See Basil Pennington, *Daily We Touch Him* (Garden City, NY: Doubleday, 1977), and *Centering Prayer* (Garden City, NY: Doubleday, 1979). Multiple resources are available from Contemplative Outreach of Colorado, http://www.contemplativeoutreach-co.org/.

the practice of the mantra. Realizing that this way of prayer could further the search of many modern people for a deeper spiritual life, he recommended two regular daily periods of meditation to be integrated with the usual practices of Christian life."[14]

What happens during those periods of meditation? One repeats the sacred word *Maranatha*. This Aramaic word is used by Saint Paul at the end of the First Letter to the Corinthians (16:22) and means "Come, Lord" or "Lord, come." The word is found in the earliest Christian liturgies and at the end of the Book of Revelation, the conclusion of the entire New Testament. If the syllables are divided slightly differently, *Maranatha* means "The Lord is here," but in Christian Meditation it is understood as "Come, Lord Jesus." One does not think about its meaning during meditation but simply repeats the distinct syllables "Ma-ra-na-tha."

Both Centering Prayer and Christian Meditation are forms of prayer based on ancient Christian texts. They were rediscovered and repackaged by monks in our time and may beneficially be used by monks and nuns, as well as lay people. Their use remains optional, since individuals have differing needs and preferences when it comes to forms of prayer.

The Jesus Prayer

Monastic tradition, especially in the East, has made use of the Jesus Prayer since the early Middle Ages. It is a composite formula drawn from passages of the gospels and centered on the name of Jesus. The full Jesus Prayer is "Lord Jesus Christ, son of God, have mercy on me, a sinner." In the Eastern Church this prayer gradually came to be esteemed until, by the ninth century, it was the predominant short prayer in use.[15] The Jesus Prayer was practiced with great fidelity in the Hesychastic monastic tradition, especially on Mount Athos since the fourteenth century.

---

[14] WCCM, http://www.wccm.org/content/john-main.

[15] For an historical and theological study of the Jesus Prayer see Irénée Hausherr, *The Name of Jesus*, trans. Charles Cummings, CS 44 (Kalamazoo, MI: Cistercian Publications, 1978).

Hesychasts pursue inner stillness (*hesychia*) and union with God by recitation of the Jesus Prayer.

The story of an anonymous nineteenth-century Russian peasant, *The Way of a Pilgrim*, has done much to spread the practice of the Jesus Prayer in the West. The pilgrim learned this prayer from a *staretz*, or spiritual father, who told him, "The continuous interior prayer of Jesus is a constant uninterrupted calling on the divine Name of Jesus with the lips, in the spirit, in the heart." The pilgrim set off on his travels saying, "Lord Jesus Christ, have mercy on me." In time the prayer passed from his lips to his heart, and eventually he became a walking prayer as the words seemed to repeat themselves automatically, day and night. He felt himself in harmony with God and with all creation: "Everything drew me to love and thank God: people, trees, plants, animals. I saw them all as my kinsfolk. I found in all of them the magic of the Name of Jesus."[16] The "pilgrim's way" was not only the trail he followed through the Russian countryside but, far more, the practice of ceaseless, interior prayer of the heart focused on the saving name of Jesus.

The first half of the Jesus Prayer, "Lord Jesus Christ, son of God," expresses our faith in Christ's divine sonship and refers to the mystery of his human life on earth. The second half, "have mercy on me, a sinner," acknowledges our faults and puts us into a living relationship with the power of God's healing, redeeming love. Thus the Jesus Prayer encapsulates the Gospel and its fundamental message of incarnation and redemption.

When we repeat the Jesus Prayer, we call down mercy upon ourselves but also upon the whole human family with whom we stand in solidarity, both in sinfulness and in redemption. Like Saint Paul, we feel the suffering and sin of the world as our own (2 Cor 11:29-30), and when we pray for mercy all humanity prays within us. We are bonded with the rest of humanity like branches on the vine that is Christ, whether we are explicitly aware of it or not. From the desert tradition, the writer and teacher Evagrius

---

[16] Anonymous, *The Way of a Pilgrim and The Pilgrim Continues His Way*, trans. R. M. French (New York: Ballantine Books, 1974), 6, 78.

(346–399) said, "A monk is a man who is separated from all and who is in harmony with all. A monk is a man who considers himself one with all men because he seems constantly to see himself in every man."[17]

Since the Jesus Prayer is a plea for mercy, is it still meaningful to repeat this prayer when we become aware of having received God's mercy? In such a case we may choose to continue repeating the Jesus Prayer, knowing that we pray it on behalf of all who are still in need of God's mercy. Or we may adopt a new formula that reflects our feelings of gratitude, joy, and love. It is also possible to give the Jesus Prayer an implicit new meaning: "Have mercy on me a sinner, as you always do."

Short Prayers in Practice

The ideal of continual prayer has not been lost over the centuries and is still cherished by many Christians, both Eastern and Western. Today there is great freedom in the choice of a formula. A verse, even a single word, that makes a special impression when heard during the liturgy or during *lectio divina* may become one's short prayer for the day. For a more systematic use of short prayers, an unchanging formula may be selected and used over a long period of time.

The prayer we choose should be personally satisfying, fit one's stage of spiritual growth, and emphasize praise, love, healing, or redemption. It may be a verse from the Psalms or elsewhere in the Bible or the liturgy, or it may be a prayer of one's own devising. Some look for a prayer of seven syllables, because this number is thought to correspond to internal rhythms of heartbeat and breathing.[18] Examples are: "*Kyrie eleison*," "*Maranatha* O Lord come," "Jesus Mary and Joseph," "Jesus healer make me whole,"

---

[17] Evagrius Ponticus, chaps. 124–25, in *Praktikos and Chapters on Prayer*, 2nd ed., trans. John Eudes Bamberger, CS 4 (Kalamazoo, MI: Cistercian Publications, 1972), 76.

[18] For instruction on seven-syllable prayer, see chap. 1 in Linda Sabbath, *The Radiant Heart* (Denville, NJ: Dimension Books, 1977).

"All my being bless the Lord," "Not my will but yours be done." Other people may prefer a prayer of one short word that sums up their desire to surrender to the Lord. The saving name of Jesus is a particularly powerful prayer. More examples are "Abba," "Love," "Amen," "Alleluia," "Father," "Savior," "Mercy."[19]

How are short prayers to be said? Adaptable to many situations, they can be repeated, peacefully and unhurriedly, as we walk down a hallway, drive along the freeway, wait for something to begin, change clothes, or occupy ourselves in a form of manual labor that does not demand our full attention all the time. Short prayers can also be used during a period of meditation as a kind of background refrain. A knotted string or a string of beads passed over the fingers may facilitate repetition. There is no daily quota of short prayers to get through in a compulsive way. Instead there is total freedom to pray in simplicity, whether aloud or mentally, in a tranquil, rhythmic fashion.

It may be helpful to coordinate praying with breathing by saying part of the prayer while inhaling and the remainder while exhaling. The body is thus brought into the prayer so that the whole person prays in a unity of body, mind, and heart. Saint John Climacus, a sixth-century monk, advocated this practice when he wrote: "Let remembrance of Jesus be present with your every breath. Then indeed you will appreciate the value of stillness (*hesychia*)."[20] The Hesychasts thought of breathing as the natural path to the heart; they tried to draw their prayer and their mind down into their heart with every breath. In their heart, at

---

[19] The author of *The Cloud of Unknowing* recommends a short prayer of one syllable. He is confident that a short prayer pierces heaven, as when we hear someone shouting "help" or "fire" and instinctively respond to this one-syllable cry. The author suggests repeating the word "sin" or "God." He writes, "Lift up your heart, therefore, with a blind stirring of love, thinking of sin and God. You are seeking God and hoping to be rid of sin. . . . Try to strike down all your knowing and feeling of everything under God, and tread everything down far beneath the cloud of forgetting" (*The Cloud of Unknowing*, trans. Ira Progoff [New York: The Julian Press, 1957], 158–59).

[20] John Climacus, *The Ladder of Divine Ascent* 27, trans. Colm Luibheid (Mahwah, NJ: Paulist Press, 1982), 269.

the center of their being, they experienced *hesychia*—deep stillness, rest, harmony, wholeness, and tranquility.[21]

Going from Prayers to Prayer

Short prayers, whether coordinated with breathing or not, help to silence the interior clamor of mind and heart. The most difficult obstacle to silence is not the tongue but the thoughts that spontaneously begin to rise from the unconscious as soon as we stop speaking or reading or concentrating on the present occupation. Repetitive short prayers give the mind something to occupy its attention, thus reducing distractions. The prayer focuses the mind and prevents it from wandering easily in various directions. The prayer itself is verbal and in that sense a noise, a little like white noise, but it is an ordered, deliberate noise that enables us to quiet other noises and listen on a deeper level.

A short prayer is like music playing in the background while we concentrate on working or studying; the prayer in the background tends to occupy the surface level of the mind and helps us to concentrate on a deeper level. The formula itself is a vocal prayer that is beneficial, but its further value is to free the heart for a deeper prayer that consists in silent listening to the Lord in spirit and in truth. The repeated formula forms a curtain of words behind which God can be encountered in the holy of holies where he dwells in the depths of my heart.

There is some evidence that not only prayers but any phrase or *mantra*, whether meaningful or not, will have the same physiological and psychological effect if it is repeated over and over again.[22] Consequently, while repeating a short meaningful vocal prayer, we do not always need to advert consciously to the

---

[21] Instruction on Hesychast spirituality and prayer of the heart can be found in *The Philokalia* vols. 1–4, trans. G. E. H. Palmer, P. Sherrard, and K. Ware (New York: Macmillan, 1983).

[22] See Herbert Benson, *The Relaxation Response* (New York: William Morrow, 1975), 113. The relaxation response is triggered by repeating a sound or gazing fixedly at an object while seated in a comfortable position in a quiet environment, without encouraging or pursuing distractions. The findings

meaning of the words. Just as when saying the rosary one need only to meditate on the mysteries instead of on the words of the Hail Mary, so when saying a short prayer we repeat the words while listening for the gentle murmur of the Spirit who dwells in our hearts. We may say, with the Russian pilgrim, that the prayer is repeating itself in our heart, reverberating endlessly in our heart, saying itself within us. The repetition becomes a reverberation more than a communication and draws us into harmony with the enveloping Divine Presence. The important thing is not the words but the heart awakening to love.

Perhaps the mind will cease repeating the words of the prayer. No matter. If the heart goes on being attentive to God, the verbal formula has done its work and is no longer needed. When our listening presence to the Lord is disturbed by foreign thoughts or feelings, it is time to return again to the conscious repetition of our prayer formula. The prayer will direct our awareness inward, reawakening the heart once again. Hesychastic monks spoke of this movement as the leading of the mind down into the heart by means of the breath-prayer.

Distractions are to be expected. Consciousness is an almost incessant cascade of images, words, emotions, sensations. Short prayers are a powerful psychological instrument for disengaging ourselves from this stream of consciousness. Whenever distractions come, like flotsam in the stream, we can always go back to our prayer and let the thoughts drift past without detaining them for further consideration. The Hesychastic tradition recommends never getting involved with passing thoughts, never stopping to analyze them. Usually the thoughts will drift by as casually as they first appeared if we are faithful to our prayer formula. The attitude taken toward distractions is almost one of passivity, letting them come and go, not becoming anxious about them and thus prolonging them.

---

of researchers indicate that using almost any word or phrase as a *mantra*, even the word *one*, will produce the physiological response of relaxation.

Conclusion

The practice of short prayers is helpful and laudable, but it is only a means and not the whole of monastic life. God cannot be contained in words. Jesus himself cautioned us, "Not everyone who says to me, 'Lord, Lord,' will enter the kingdom of heaven but only the one who does the will of my Father in heaven" (Matt 7:21). Doing God's will is a matter of living in faith, hope, and love "with joy from the Holy Spirit" (1 Thess 1:6). We do well to repeat short prayers as long as they find an expression in the way we live, that is, in our response to the call of love in every situation and in our willingness to take up our cross daily in imitation of Jesus. Sanctity does not depend on knowing the words of a holy formula. That would be magic. The author of the Second Epistle to Timothy tells us the one thing we should depend on: "This saying is trustworthy: If we have died with him we shall live with him; if we persevere we shall also reign with him" (2 Tim 2:11-12).

Saint Benedict reminded his disciples that they stand in the presence of God continually, whether they are explicitly praying or not: "We believe that the divine presence is everywhere and 'that in every place the eyes of the Lord are watching the good and the wicked'" (RB 19.1 quoting Prov 15:3). Prayer is the turning of our mind and heart to God present everywhere. Short prayers are intended to awaken our heart and keep it lovingly attentive to our Beloved.

Expressed by a prudent practice of short prayers, continual prayer resembles a relationship of intimate friendship or the love of a husband for his wife or of a mother for her children. The mother of three grown children compared her practice of continual prayer to maternal love in this way: "I guess the only way I can express it," she wrote, "is that, like the love for one's children, it is always there, regardless of one's activities . . . sometimes stronger than others, but never a time when it is not present. And what is prayer if it is not love?" Short prayers are one of the monastic practices for awakening the heart to a life of continual love.

Questions for Reflection

What similarities and differences do you see between Christian Meditation and Centering Prayer?

What meanings do you find in Sr. Bernarda's drawing at the beginning of this chapter? Hint: study Psalm 45:1.

with
expanded
HEARTS
we run
THE WAY

we do it for a crown that will never fade

SELF-DISCIPLINE

In today's free and permissive society, monastic self-discipline is countercultural. We monks have found, however, a secret path to freedom in self-discipline. The word *discipline*, from the Latin *disciplina*, meaning "instruction," suggests an attitude of listening and learning, an attitude of discipleship. The monastery is "a school for the Lord's service" (RB Prol. 45),[1] and the Holy Spirit is our schoolmaster. "Where the Spirit of the Lord is, there is freedom," Saint Paul assures us (2 Cor 3:17). The Spirit calls us to make a free gift of self that conforms us to the dying and rising Christ. Everyone who loses his or her life for the sake of the gospel becomes gradually more compassionate, more open, freer, more human, more in the image and likeness of the Risen Christ. First, there must be the radical giving and losing of self, the full surrender of our selves into the hands of God.

[1] *The Rule of Saint Benedict 1980,* ed. Timothy Fry (Collegeville, MN: Liturgical Press, 1981), 165.

The term *self-discipline* points to self as the object to be disciplined. Self is also the subject, the one who disciplines, but only in cooperation with divine grace. We are not trying to be our own savior. History gives examples of individuals who have gotten carried away by the challenge of self-discipline, as if they were going for the gold medal in an Olympic sport. They become fierce athletes of renunciation and mortification. Instead we always need to remember that our spiritual liberation and transformation are gifts of grace and not our own personal achievements. Those who freely and cheerfully follow the Lord down the path of renunciation discover that his yoke is indeed easy and his burden truly light (Matt 11:30).

Those who choose the monastic way of life know that they have accepted a lifestyle with considerable built-in discipline. Saying *yes* to monastic life includes a *no* to many legitimate human activities and potentials, for example, parenthood. People who are fresh from a culture that gives high value to the full actualization of one's potential will feel monastic renunciations keenly. In fact, however, a *yes* to one's vocational choice includes a *no* to other possible options; one who eats his cake renounces the possibility of still having it. A person entering one of our monasteries does give up part of his or her human potentiality. There are not only the renunciations involved in the vows but also other deprivations that are demanding, especially if they seem to imply giving up the exercise of our God-given, creative gifts and talents. These are the concrete expressions of the radical giving and losing of self that takes place in monastic life.

Perfection does not consist in bodily penances and self-inflicted pain under the name of renunciation or mortification. It is a false spirituality that says, "If it hurts, it's holy." Pain for the sake of pain does not please God. Finding pleasure in self-inflicted suffering suggests a psychological abnormality called masochism. Can we then justify the opposite extreme, a narcissistic, hedonistic self-indulgence in the name of freedom? No, because pampering the body, yielding to all its desires, hinders spiritual attainment and eventually harms bodily health as well. Athletes and dancers who expect their bodies to accomplish difficult feats are obliged to discipline themselves strictly (see 1 Cor 9:25-27). Shall I then expect to be a contemplative and a gourmand at the same time?

In our day, some people look for gurus to teach them a technique that will produce religious experience without any preliminary ascetical preparation. Mystical ecstasy can be pursued like any other sensate thrill, in order to increase personal pleasure. Yet the entire tradition of monasticism bears witness that union with God in the highest state of consciousness usually presupposes a program of self-discipline rather than of self-indulgence. Everything comes with a price tag; a strong love is willing to pay the price. The human price tag on the contemplative encounter with God is persevering self-discipline, except in cases of extraordinary, divine intervention.

Motivated Self-Discipline

I may accept the general necessity of shouldering my cross and following in the footsteps of the crucified Christ, but when it comes to concrete practices of monastic self-discipline, such as fasting, my motivation begins to flag. It is always possible to find excuses for not practicing self-discipline in particular circumstances. Underlying my hesitation may be a genuine confusion about the proper motive for self-discipline. Even the example of Jesus is somewhat ambiguous. Jesus fasted in the desert (Matt 4:2), but his customary practice was to eat and drink freely from whatever was available. Jesus was not an ascetic like John the Baptist: "John appeared neither eating nor drinking, and people say, 'He is mad!' The Son of Man appeared eating and drinking, and they say, 'This one is a glutton and drunkard'" (Matt 11:18-19). If Jesus was not an ascetic, why should monks and nuns be concerned about ascetical practices?

There are several possible motives or reasons for ascetic self-discipline. I will review four of them and evaluate them globally after all four have been presented. Any one of these could be someone's conscious or unconscious motivation for self-discipline.

Body Fitness. If personal fitness is my motive, I discipline my bodily appetites in order to achieve an integrated state of self-realization, a healthy mind in a healthy body. I practice self-discipline in order to keep my body in shape, as an expert mechanic might fine-tune a carburetor for top performance. If my body is out of tune, I grow flabby and fat. Exercise and periodic fasting are good for the body and will increase my chances for a long, productive life. Fasting, for example, is a natural purgative that eliminates salt, acid crystals, cholesterols, and other toxic substances that accumulate in an overloaded digestive system. I do not live to eat but eat to live and to function as an integrated, self-actualized human being. When I am in top shape, my body itself will be an honor to God. I will be glorifying and praising God with and by my fine-tuned, carefully maintained body (see 1 Cor 6:20).

Anti-Materiality. This motive is not common, but Gnosticism is not entirely extinct. "God is spirit," Jesus assures us (John 4:24). I may reason that in order to be united with God I must become as spiritual as possible by abstaining from material things, especially pleasurable things. If something feels good, I will try to deny myself that pleasure, thus putting to death my passions and bodily desires. When I have systematically ruled all material joys out of my life, God alone will be my joy. The aim of my asceticism is to shake off the dust and defilement of material things and so purify my heart. I advance in the spiritual life by progressively denying myself and restricting myself to the minimum use of material things. Nothing created can unite me with the uncreated God. Only the spirit is willing and able; the flesh is weak and unreliable (see Matt 26:41). Spirit can prevail and direct my life only when matter and flesh have been virtually annihilated. By self-discipline I reduce the hold that materiality has on me and I stretch myself out spirit-thin until I become transparent to the divine light, absorbed in the divine light.

Redirection of Forces. In this scenario the flesh is not to be annihilated, suppressed, stamped out, but instead reordered, transformed, sublimated, divinized. The body has tremendous energy at its disposal, the energy of passion. By careful self-discipline I can rechannel this energy to serve a higher purpose, instead of trying to short-circuit it. If prayer is my main purpose in the monastery, then everything in me has to be ordered to that supreme interest, even if it means sweat and tears for the flesh. "No one can serve two masters" (Matt 6:24). With a total gift of self, I have chosen to serve Christ crucified, and therefore I have to take pains to see that nothing diverts me from his service or interferes with the primacy of my love for him. "Taking pains" is another way of saying "doing penance." I am ready to take all the pains necessary to unify and center my whole self on Christ crucified and glorified.

Liberation through Discipline. The more I try to make Christ the center of my life, thoughts, and actions, the more I feel every pull and tug that draws me back from the radical, loving surrender of myself. I am not totally free to run toward the one I love. Instead I feel enchained, entangled by a thousand little threads that together form a strong rope binding me to myself. Detaching myself from these bonds is largely a matter of self-discipline and asceticism. Paradoxically, self-discipline sets me free for God. Self-discipline is training in freedom. I am free to take something comfortable and pleasurable, free to eat and drink more, free to sleep longer, but I am also free to refrain from these things and not let myself be held bound by them. True Christian freedom is the freedom of those who live no longer for themselves, the freedom of being a new creation in Christ (2 Cor 5:15, 17). The movement of self-discipline leads out of bondage to the self into an experience of newness and freedom, then back again to a liberated use, appreciation, and enjoyment of material goods, in moderation, without becoming entangled again by a thousand little threads.

From the not entirely unbiased description of these four possible motives for self-discipline, it is already evident that the fourth alternative offers the most viable and life-giving approach. Monastic self-discipline is a subtle technique for liberation of flesh and spirit, proceeding with firmness but not with a heavy-handed repression that would try to extinguish human feelings and emotions or to refuse all use of material goods. Nor does self-discipline fall to the seduction of body-sculpting; instead it attunes the whole self to hear the deeper calls and values of life in Christ. The Holy Spirit always calls us to move beyond ourselves in loving response to others.

At first it may seem that the requirements of the spiritual life destroy freedom, but in fact they are in the service of true freedom. This principle holds in every field of excellence. Time and persistent, self-imposed discipline are keys to a mastery that can be creatively free. Dance instructor Martha Graham has said of her art, "Your goal is freedom, but freedom may only be achieved through discipline. In the studio you learn to conform, to submit yourself to the demands of your craft so that you may finally be free."[2]

Self-Discipline in Externals

Before setting out the prescriptions of his Rule, Saint Benedict apologizes in his Prologue for "a little strictness," although he hopes to set down "nothing harsh, nothing burdensome" (RB Prol 46–47). As in all life, a certain difficulty is inevitable in monastic life. The first form of monastic self-discipline is cheerfully and generously to accept the inevitable harshness of life and to endure the difficulties that come our way in the course of each day, whether from the observance of rules or from circumstances. Only secondarily does monastic self-discipline consist in voluntarily chosen penances or works of supererogation.

Living by the common rule of the monastery, in close quarters with minimal privacy, often demands considerable self-discipline. The customs of the house usually do not provide those moments of gratification that enable people outside the monastery to get through the day—the morning and afternoon break, the evening drink to relax, the satisfying cigarette after meals. Breaking these habits of legitimate indulgence may require great self-discipline of the newcomer. In addition, there is the adjustment to using things that everybody else uses, instead of having things for one's exclusive personal use. Poverty and the common

---

[2] As found in Edward Fischer, *Everybody Steals from God* (Notre Dame, IN: University of Notre Dame Press, 1977), 56; also found in Joshua Spodek, "A master speaks on creative expression," blog, http://joshuaspodek.com /master-speaks-creative-expression.

life are penitential in themselves, as one soon discovers when he or she makes a practice of using articles of clothing from the common supply, common plates and cups from the kitchen, tools from the common tool room, a bicycle or pick-up left for common use. Usually we do not need to go looking for penances. They come to us. Our brothers or sisters often bring us our penances. All we have to do is accept, with a willing, cheerful spirit, what comes to us each day.

Saint John of the Cross spells out the principles of voluntary, external self-discipline in the following maxims:

> Endeavor to be inclined always: not to the easiest, but to the most difficult; not to the most delightful, but to the harshest; not to the most gratifying, but to the less pleasant; not to what means rest for you, but to hard work; not to the consoling, but to the unconsoling; not to the most, but to the least; not to the highest and most precious, but to the lowest and most despised; not to wanting something, but to wanting nothing; do not go about looking for the best of temporal things, but for the worst, and desire to enter into complete nudity, emptiness and poverty in everything in the world.[3]

Here the call to a radical giving and losing of self comes through like a clarion. John's eye was on the crucified Christ, stripped and naked on the cross.

For us, the Carmelite's maxims have to be implemented not in one grand, heroic act of martyrdom but in a multitude of ordinary, everyday circumstances. There is the self-discipline we can practice in the area of fraternal charity, when we listen graciously to someone who is a little too talkative and tiresome. Or we may be assigned to work with someone whose personality, idiosyncrasies, and style of working grate unceasingly on our nerves. And yet we will find a way to show respect and compassion and maintain

---

[3] John of the Cross, *Ascent of Mount Carmel* 1.13.6, trans. Kieran Kavanaugh and Otilio Rodríguez, *The Collected Works of St. John of the Cross* (Washington, DC: Institute of Carmelite Studies, 1973), 102.

a loving attitude of openness toward him or her. Self-discipline shows itself in accepting the limitations of others, including superiors, as they accept our limitations. To live with and accept our own spiritual, intellectual, psychological, and bodily limitations is already an asceticism, especially as we grow older and feel the diminishment of our powers on all levels.

Over and above these forms of self-discipline, we might feel called to deny ourselves in one or another of a dozen little ways that no one else can see. These personal forms of penance might include skipping for a day the reading of the newspaper, sitting without crossing the legs, standing when I would prefer to sit, not opening a letter from home until the next day, enduring the heat of summer and the cold of winter, not leaning back against the stalls when standing in choir, attending and actively participating in community meetings, and eating food I do not care for rather than "fasting" from it. Literal fasting from food remains an effective form of monastic self-discipline.

Fasting and Abstinence

Fasting has a biblical foundation as an expression of humble dependence on the Lord. To fast with the idea of compelling God to do our will is foreign to genuine biblical spirituality.[4] Jesus did not command his disciples to fast (Mark 2:18), but neither did he forbid it to anyone who could fast with the right motive, without ostentation (Mark 2:20; Matt 6:16-18).

Fasting is denying oneself nourishment, either totally or in part, for a definite length of time. A water fast, for example, consists in fasting from everything but water with perhaps a little

---

[4] In the gospel scene where Jesus casts out a deaf and dumb demon that his disciples were unable to expel, Jesus explains, "This kind can only come out through prayer" (Mark 9:29). Prayer is an expression of faith in God's power. Some of our monastic fathers followed a version of Scripture that added the words "by prayer and fasting," but this addition, assigning a special power to fasting, is lacking in the best manuscripts and is not accepted as authentic by modern editors. Matthew 17:21 is based on Mark 9:29 and is likewise rejected as spurious in critical editions.

honey and lemon juice added, for twenty-four or thirty-six hours. A fruit-juice fast consists in fasting from everything but fruit juice for a certain period. People in normal health are ordinarily capable of this kind of fasting from time to time. Nevertheless, for some it would be prudent to check first with a health worker (see RB 49:8-9). Care should be taken when breaking these total fasts, especially if they are prolonged. Raw vegetables are recommended for the first solid food, followed by cooked vegetables, and then by such protein sources as dairy products, eggs, grains, and nuts.

More common than prolonged total fasting in our monasteries is partial fasting. The Rule of Saint Benedict prescribes an ordinary monastic fast from September 14 until Ash Wednesday (RB 41.6). In our time, this monastic fast might consist of a light evening meal if the main meal is taken at noon. The same custom of partial fasting could be observed during Lent. On two days in Lent, Ash Wednesday and Good Friday, we could be content with bread and water at the principal meal.

In recent years there has been a decreased tendency to impose fasting on the entire community, although some communities may, by consensus, designate a particular day each month as a day of fasting. More and more, the degree and frequency of fasting has been left to the responsible judgment of each individual. Food is provided or available, but the individual is free to fast if he or she wishes. Cooks do not have the obligation of imposing fasts on the community but of preparing nourishing, tasty, balanced meals that individuals may partake of or fast from as they wish.

Variations of partial fasting on particular days might include skipping a meal, skipping dessert, omitting sweetener in coffee or jam on toast, being content with a single portion or with small servings of several portions, limiting oneself to one breakfast and not taking a midmorning coffee break, getting along without snacks between meals. Fasting is a matter of discretion as well as of inclination and grace. There is an appropriate time for fasting and an appropriate time for feasting; discretion would suggest that we feast, not fast, on feast days.

What are some of the results and benefits of fasting? Fasting helps me to appreciate food as God's gift and teaches me to hunger for spiritual nourishment as much as I hunger for food and drink. As I fast, I might increase the time I devote to sacred reading: "Not on bread alone is man to live, but on every utterance that comes from the mouth of God" (Matt 4:4; Deut 8:3). Fasting may train me in using only what I really need in life and using it with reverence and gratefulness.[5] Further, when I know what it feels like to be truly hungry, there is a lived experience of solidarity with the famine-stricken, starving people of the world. I also experience a nearness to the mystery of Jesus fasting in the desert for forty days in the tradition of Moses and Elijah. Humble fasting opens the heart in preparation for encountering God as did Moses on Sinai and Elijah on Horeb. Even psychologically, fasting seems to result in a mental clarity favorable to prayer and an openness to insights, intuition, and inspiration, although this plateau of clarity may not come until after the headache stage that is the body's usual first reaction to withdrawal from its customary stimulants of food and drink.

Abstinence from meat, that is, vegetarianism, may be considered a form of fasting, a fasting from "the meat of four-footed animals," as Saint Benedict prescribes (RB 39.11). He suggests no particular motive for vegetarianism because he is imposing a practice already taken for granted by monastic tradition. In later centuries, the practice fell out of use. In fact, it was to some extent vegetarianism that led to the split in the Cistercian Order between the Strict Observance and the Common Observance in the seventeenth century. As with any such custom, the practice of monastic vegetarianism may be critically reviewed and modifications introduced if they are indicated. Even Saint Benedict considers good health to be a higher value, for he permits meat to be served to the sick (RB 39.11).

Monastic families that retain the observance of vegetarianism, whether always or at certain seasons, might reflect on their reasons.

---

[5] For a development of this idea see Basil Pennington, "Fasting: A Fundamental Christian Attitude," *Review for Religious* 36 (September 1977): 729–33.

In our culture, because meat is the common and preferred fare, abstaining from it is considered a privation. A case is sometimes made for a vegetarian diet on the grounds of better health. The claim can be disputed, but at least there is no reason why any important nutrients need be missing from a well-planned vegetarian menu. On other grounds, some in our time are turning away from meat as a symbolic statement of their commitment to nonviolence. To sustain one's life on the life of weaker animals is considered a violent way to live. We may note in the book of Genesis that the first account of creation (Gen 1:29-30) presumed that all animals, including human beings, were vegetarians and lived harmoniously in a peaceful kingdom (Isa 11:6-9). After the fall and the flood, God explicitly permitted the consumption of flesh meat (Gen 9:3).[6]

In the climate of freedom inaugurated with the new covenant, we know that "everything is indeed clean" (Rom 14:20) and that "the kingdom of God is not a matter of food and drink, but of righteousness, peace, and joy in the holy Spirit" (Rom 14:17). If our practice of vegetarianism is found to be healthier or more symbolic or more economical than eating meat, these are not benefits that necessarily bring us closer to God. "We are no worse off if we do not eat, nor are we better off if we do," says Saint Paul in a discussion about eating meat sacrificed to idols and later sold at the market (1 Cor 8:8). Instead of playing off the supposed value of one practice against the other, Saint Paul grounded both practices in the radical Christian obligation to honor God and avoid offending the conscience of others (1 Cor 8:13; Rom 14:20). The self-discipline involved in our practice of partial or total vegetarianism finds a satisfactory motive in the Benedictine principle of glorifying God in all things (RB 57.8; cf. 1 Pet 4:11). The controversies that have surrounded this practice in the course of monastic history can be transcended in the light of higher values: "Whoever eats, eats for the Lord, since he gives thanks to God; while whoever abstains, abstains for the Lord and gives thanks to God" (Rom 14:6).

---

[6] See Bruce Vawter, *On Genesis* (Garden City, NY: Doubleday, 1977), 60, 133.

Interior Self-Discipline

I have been discussing forms of self-discipline that involve the renunciation of such external things as food and bodily comforts. Monastic self-discipline goes deeper. Typically we move from externals to the interior; that is, first we discipline the body and then, through the body, the spirit. Saint Maximus the Confessor (580–662) writes, "He who has renounced things, as women, money, and the like, makes a monk of the outer man, but not yet of the inner. He that renounces the impassioned representations of these same things makes a monk of the inner man, that is, of the mind. It is easy to make a monk of the outer man, if only one wants to; but it is no little struggle to make a monk of the inner man."[7]

Interior self-discipline is a deeper and harder practice, because it affects us on the level of our ego. Interior self-discipline aims at liberating and transforming us at the root of our desires and defenses. It aims at purity of heart, without which one cannot see God or be united to God. "Blessed are the clean of heart, for they will see God" (Matt 5:8). Self-discipline facilitates our conformity to Christ so that we learn to judge, perceive, think, and value as Jesus does. Over the months and years we spend in the monastery, faithful to exterior practices of self-discipline, grace is slowly converting us, changing our mind and heart, turning us away from the worldly, ego-centered values we once lived by (for instance, to get rich, to look good, to be popular, to be in charge and tell others what to do, to enjoy some of the creature comforts that make life sweet).

Saint Benedict's stress on humility in chapter 7 of the Rule is fundamental to the interior transformation that happens in the monastery. If you find a monk or nun who has lived monastic life for many years and is humble, gentle, loving, willing to help, ready to give up his or her own plans and preferences for the sake of the community, then you find someone who has attained, with the help of God's grace, the interior self-discipline that our exterior self-discipline aims at.

[7] Maximus the Confessor, *The Ascetic Life: The Four Centuries on Charity* 4.50, trans. Polycarp Sherwood, Ancient Christian Writers, vol. 21 (Westminster, MD: Newman Press, 1955), 199.

Saint Maximus saw the need of renouncing the "impassioned representations" that fill the mind and heart. These are the products of unfulfilled desire. Monastic self-discipline involves the death of desire. Renunciation and self-discipline on the exterior level are meant to extinguish gradually our inordinate desires and appetites. Saint John of the Cross considers this distinction highly important: "We are not discussing the mere lack of things; this lack will not divest the soul if it craves for all these objects. We are dealing with the denudation of the soul's appetites. . . . The things of the world . . . are not in themselves an encumbrance or harm to [the soul]; rather it is the will and appetite dwelling within it that causes the damage."[8]

Interior self-discipline grapples with our habitual, voluntary, inordinate loves and cravings and gives us in their place monastic values: the love of silence, solitude, prayer, reading, manual labor, and simplicity. Transformation of the inner self implies turning away from the worldly, ego-centered values we once lived by and embracing the monastic path to God. With interior self-discipline comes a shift in consciousness away from the past toward the present moment of salvation. As we draw away from our past we initially feel uprooted, lonely, depressed, or bored, until we get our feet on the new ground of monastic living and complete that radical shift in our ways of judging, perceiving, thinking, valuing.

Newcomers to monastic life may feel keenly their separation from their former way of life, their family and friends. Homesickness can be a purifying form of self-discipline, especially on days of family get-togethers like Christmas and Thanksgiving. A common way of deadening the pain of distancing ourselves from the past, and a way of slowing down the work of interior transformation, is to reminisce about the past. Such daydreams can be an escape from the present demands of monastic living. Dreamy introspection is the last refuge of what Saint Maximus calls "impassioned representations" and Saint John of the Cross calls "the soul's appetites." With the continual aid of divine grace,

[8] John of the Cross, *Ascent* 1.3, in *Collected Works*, 77.

our past will be healed and integrated into our present as self-discipline slowly molds us both exteriorly and interiorly.

Genuine Self-Discipline

There are signs by which we can recognize whether our self-discipline is inspired by grace and is accomplishing what it is intended to accomplish. I will consider three of these signs.

Heart of Flesh. Perseverance in monastic self-discipline should soften the heart of a monk or nun and make it pliable in the hands of the divine potter who shapes him or her into the living image of Christ. Our asceticism is misguided if it makes us hardened, insensitive, inhuman, impenetrable individualists who stubbornly refuse to drop our defenses. Spontaneous reactions to unexpected circumstances provide clues to our inner dispositions. How do we react to being corrected or humiliated? If we accept these experiences as God's will and allow them to soften our heart, we are likely to be on the right road. On the contrary, if we become defensive, blame others, even plan to get even, then we are losing the way. Our penitential exercises should teach us to mistrust our own strength and rely entirely on God, surrendering the control of our life to him. Renunciation gives us a taste of our nothingness and creates room in us for God to act. Exterior asceticism is oriented to purity, pliability of heart, and humility. Gradually our heart of stone is transformed into a heart of flesh and conformed to the heart of Jesus crucified, who always did what pleased his Father (see Ezek 36:26).

Joyfulness. In the "Decree on Religious Life," the Second Vatican Council described communities entirely dedicated to contemplation. These communities occupy themselves with God alone "in solitude and silence, with constant prayer and penance willingly undertaken [*alacri poenitentia*]."[9] The concluding phrase, applicable to all Christian self-discipline, describes a practice of penance that is not only ready and willing but also cheerful.

---

[9] Second Vatican Council, *Perfectae Caritatis* no. 7, http://www.vatican
.va/archive/hist_councils/ii_vatican_council/documents/vat-ii_decree
_19651028_perfectae-caritatis_en.html.

Penances that are shouldered reluctantly, with gloomy looks and groans, probably do not touch the deep root of inordinate desire. Penances offered to God with a glad heart and a cheerful, smiling countenance are more fruitful and effective. Jesus himself said, "When you fast, do not look gloomy like the hypocrites. . . . But when you fast, anoint your head and wash your face" (Matt 6:16-17).[10] The healthy monastic attitude toward self-discipline is to embrace it, not simply to tolerate or endure it. John Cassian's concluding *Conference*, "On Mortification," devotes an entire chapter to explaining how Christ's yoke is easy and his burden truly light (Cassian, *Conferences* 24.24). The quality of community life would quickly deteriorate if our fasting and other penances made us grouchy, moody, touchy, and quick to snap at others, instead of making us more loving, compassionate, and cheerful persons.

Discretion. In his chapter on "The Measure of Drink," Saint Benedict quotes 1 Corinthians 7:7: "Everyone has his own gift from God, one this and another that" (RB 40.1). The measure of penance freely undertaken by each person should correspond to the degree of grace he or she has been given as a personal gift from God. One's desire to fast on bread and water for an extended period may be praiseworthy in itself, but it may also belong to a spiritually higher level than one has attained. Discretion would demand that one's ascetical practices correspond to one's actual spiritual and physical capability, including the capability of one's nervous and digestive systems. Otherwise the practices may actually destroy a person's health and spiritual enthusiasm. The story is told that when Saint Francis was dying, he asked pardon of his own body for having treated it so cruelly. He called his body "Brother Ass," because he forced it to carry burdens like a donkey and to eat coarse food or no food, and he beat it when it was sluggish. Cistercian history

---

[10] Compare this paraphrase: "When you practice some appetite-denying discipline to better concentrate on God, don't make a production out of it. It might turn you into a small time celebrity but it won't make you a saint. If you go into training inwardly, act normal outwardly. Shampoo and comb your hair, brush your teeth, wash your face" (Matthew 6:16-18 in Eugene H. Peterson, *The Message* [Colorado Springs, CO: NavPress, 2002], 1338).

recounts that Saint Bernard showed a lack of discretion in his excessive fasting during the early years of his monastic life.

Self-discipline also needs to be prudently in tune with a person's duties and responsibilities to the community. If fasting leaves me too weak to work, my fasting is in conflict with the practice of obedience. We know that obedience to our daily task is always better than sacrifices not asked for (1 Sam 15:22). Penance that has a detrimental effect on the way a person performs his or her assigned duties cannot be pleasing to God, who assigns those duties through the superior.

Conclusion

Living the monastic life day after day for a lifetime demands considerable self-discipline. Often there is no need to seek additional forms of penance if we simply accept the inevitable harshness and unavoidable suffering of monastic life as our share in the sufferings of Christ. Sufficient for the day, and built into the day, are the pains thereof (see Matt 6:34). These daily pains and troubles do not come from self-will; they are given to us as our daily share in the cross of Jesus. They include daily demands made on us by others or by the duties and responsibilities of our position. Jesus said that anyone who wishes to be his follower "must deny himself and take up his cross daily and follow me" (Luke 9:23).

Jesus did not choose his own cross but accepted the cup of suffering and death held out to him by his Father's hand (Luke 22:42). Simone Weil, a woman well acquainted with affliction, said, "It is not the suffering we inflict on ourselves but that which comes to us from outside which is the true remedy."[11] By accepting what comes, we surrender our own will in a radical giving and losing of self that opens for us a new dimension of humanity, in the likeness of the crucified but exalted Christ. By loving fidelity to God's will we discover the Christian paradox that "whoever would save his life will lose it, but whoever loses his

[11] Simone Weil, *Gravity and Grace* (London: Routledge and Kegan Paul, 1963), 66.

life for my sake will find it" (Matt 16:25). The daily demands of our vocation, embraced lovingly and cheerfully, can liberate the risen life of Jesus within us, as Saint Paul experienced it in his own ministry: "While we live we are constantly being delivered to death for Jesus' sake, so that the life of Jesus may be revealed in our mortal flesh" (2 Cor 4:11).

Questions for Reflection

What should be done if you become so adapted to your chosen penance that it is no longer a sacrifice to do it?

How would you respond to someone who says, "If God loves me, I do not see how it can please God to see me deliberately causing myself pain or discomfort."

at early dawn the just surrender their hearts to watching

for the Lord, and in his sight they pray

WATCHING

The night watch is a form of monastic self-discipline that deserves separate investigation because it is not easily appreciated. The custom of rising early in order to devote oneself to serious prayer and sacred reading runs counter to the living habits of people around us. Although there are exceptions, our society in general prefers to utilize the late evening hours, until midnight and beyond, rather than the early hours of the morning. The monastery is settling down for the night when most people are still up and active and is awakening when most people are enjoying their deepest sleep.

Because they have absorbed this common cultural pattern of sleeping and waking, newcomers often have difficulty adjusting to the monastic night watch and learning to be at their prime level of functioning at that time. A novice who was struggling with the difficulty of keeping awake during Vigils once asked how long it would take before he grew accustomed to being up at that hour. When told that it could easily take four or five years depending on his physical adaptability, the novice's reaction was one of evident disappointment. He felt that he could not hold out that long, and that perhaps Vigils was not worth the effort of trying to adapt.

The night watch—beginning with the time of Vigils—is not an easy practice to grow accustomed to, or to understand, or to love. For the sake of the potential spiritual benefits, are we willing to rise early and accept being sleep deprived? The monastic schedule usually allows at least seven hours of sleep, which is more than many outside the monastery can count on. How much sleep is necessary? Individual needs vary, but according to one study, the average American gets 6.8 hours but needs between 7.5 and 8 to function best.[1] Chronic sleep deprivation weakens the immune system. According to another study, sleep deprivation impairs our ability to process, recall, and retain information, while also making us touchy and grouchy.[2]

In the monastery we do not give up our night's sleep entirely, which would be watching in the strict sense, but we do rise early.[3] Rising to greet the dawn with prayer was a practice of the early Christian community. So distinctive was this Christian custom that the Roman historian Pliny, writing to the emperor Trajan in the second century, described Christians in Asia Minor as people who rise before dawn to meet in common and to sing to Christ as to a God.[4] These early Christians hoped to be awake for the Second Coming of Jesus at the end of the world. His coming might be "in the evening, at midnight, or at cockcrow, or in the

[1] Gina Shaw, "Sleep through the Decades," *WebMD*, http://www.webmd .com/sleep-disorders/features/adult-sleep-needs-and-habits.

[2] See Christy Matta, "8 Effects of Sleep Deprivation on your Health," *PsychCentral*, http://psychcentral.com/blog/archives/2013/02/13/8-effects -of-sleep-deprivation-on-your-health/.

[3] See *Constitutions and Statutes of the Monks and Nuns of the Cistercian Order of the Strict Observance* (Rome, 1990), Constitution 23: "Night Vigils. In the sober anticipation of the coming of Christ, following the tradition of the Order, the hours before sunrise are appropriately consecrated to God by the celebration of Vigils, by prayer and meditation." Statue 23.A: "The brothers'/[sisters'] hour of rising is so determined that Vigils maintains its nocturnal character."

[4] Pliny the Younger to Emperor Trajan around AD 111, http://tyrannus.com /pliny_let.html.

morning" (Mark 13:35). We have to be prepared and constantly on the watch, says Jesus, so that he does not come suddenly and catch us asleep (Mark 13:33, 36).

Two thousand years later, our expectation of the Lord's imminent return is not as strong a motive as it was for the early Christians, but monks and nuns keep that expectation alive on behalf of the whole church. They are the sentinels on the ramparts for the benefit of the whole church. They see themselves in Isaiah's description of the watchman: "On the watchtower, my Lord, I stand constantly by day; and I stay at my post through all the watches of the night" (Isa 21:8), and also: "Upon your walls, Jerusalem, I have stationed sentinels; by day and by night, they shall never be silent. You who are to remind the LORD, take no rest, and give him no rest, until he reestablishes Jerusalem and makes it the praise of the earth" (Isa 62:6-7).

The early Christian community remembered the many occasions when Jesus had urged watchfulness for the coming day of the Lord, the day the Son of Man will return. As the homeowner keeps a watchful eye against night burglars, Jesus said, "You also must be prepared" (Matt 24:44). He said that if a servant becomes negligent because he thinks his master is a long time in coming, "the servant's master will come on an unexpected day and at an unknown hour" (Matt 24:50). Since the exact day or hour of the Lord's coming is unknown, vigilance has to be constant. "Be watchful! Be alert! You do not know when the time will come. . . . What I say to you, I say to all, 'Watch'" (Mark 13:33, 36).

The watchword of the early community was, "Come, Lord Jesus!" (Rev 22:20; 1 Cor 16:22). They had committed their lives to Christ, and their hearts yearned to see him and be with him forever in his kingdom (see Phil 1:23). So they lived in a state of continual preparedness and watchfulness that found expression in the voluntary practice of praying at night. The monastic night watch expresses our own persevering expectation of the Lord's future coming and our radical orientation toward the kingdom of God. In the meantime we hold ourselves ready for the visits of the Word in prayer: "My soul yearns for you at night, yes, my spirit within me seeks you at dawn" (Isa 26:9).

Traditional Monastic Practice

Watching was a favorite ascetical practice of the desert father Arsenius: "It was also said of him that on Saturday evenings, preparing for the glory of Sunday, he would turn his back on the sun and stretch out his hands in prayer towards the heavens, till once again the sun shone on his face. Then he would sit down."[5] In the fifth century there arose an order of monks called the Acemetes, that is, "those who do not sleep." They were dedicated to perpetual recitation of the Divine Office. Of course they all had to sleep eventually, but they were organized in shifts so that their community prayer might be carried on continually, day and night. The Acemetes demonstrate that the purpose of watching is both sacrifice and intercessory prayer on behalf of the world.

John Cassian described variations of monastic vigils current in the fifth century among the monks and nuns of the Egyptian desert. The weekend communal Vigils service lasted from Friday evening throughout the night "until the fourth cockcrow." Then the monks slept for nearly two hours, rising at daybreak for Lauds and remaining awake throughout the day.[6] On other days of the week they would sleep until midnight or somewhat later, rise for the twelve psalms of Vigils, and then return to their cells for "private watchfulness" until Lauds.[7] To sleep after Vigils, they felt, would lay them open to losing "the cleanness that has been acquired by psalms and prayers" or would make them sluggish, lazy, and slothful throughout the whole day.[8]

Saint Benedict, influenced by Cassian, prescribed as follows: "In the time remaining after Vigils, those who need to learn some of the psalter or readings should study them" (RB 8.3). Benedict's

---

[5] *The Sayings of the Desert Fathers: The Alphabetical Collection* 30, trans. Benedicta Ward, CS 59 (Kalamazoo, MI: Cistercian Publications, 1975), 12.

[6] John Cassian, *Institutes* 3.8, trans. Boniface Ramsey, Ancient Christian Writers no. 58 (New York: The Newman Press, 2000), 65.

[7] Cassian, *Institutes*, 2.13, 46. The practice is described also in the previous chapter: "None of them gives in any more to reposeful sleep until, with the coming of the daylight, the day's work follows upon the night's toil and meditation" (Cassian, *Institutes* 2.12, 45).

[8] Cassian, *Institutes* 2.13, 46. See also *Institutes* 3.5, 64.

monasteries ran on a solar calendar, with longer nights and more sleep during the winter months and less during the summer. During the summer, however, a siesta was permitted after the noon meal; those who wished to do sacred reading at that time were instructed to read privately "without disturbing the others" (RB 48.5). With his concern for moderation, Benedict did not permit overindulgence in sleep, for "the sleepy like to make excuses" (RB 22.8); but even during the shorter nights of summer he wanted his monks to have enough sleep so as to "arise with their food fully digested" (RB 8.2).

Keeping awake at Vigils has always remained a struggle for many, as a story from the Cistercian tradition in the 1170s illustrates. At Clairvaux, a prior named John devised a simple and forceful mechanism to awaken him whenever he nodded off during Vigils. He fastened a hammer to the side of his choir stall in such a way that when his head dropped, the hammer would also drop and strike his tonsured dome![9] The night watch is a struggle that we feel in our own flesh and bones. We undertake it night after night not only that we ourselves might be awake for our Lord's coming but also for the sake of people throughout the world who are spiritually somnolent and asleep to the call of the Lord.

Contemporary Monastic Practice

The night watch begins with the celebration of Vigils and continues afterward in the silent darkness until the morning prayer of Lauds. The office of Vigils consecrates the hours of the night, creating a spirit of expectancy. In the quiet hours before dawn, the stillness around us pervades our minds and hearts. We wait prayerfully for the coming of the Lord as we watch and long for the coming of dawn (see Ps 130:6). We watch, for we know

---

[9] See Conrad of Eberbach, *Exordium Magnum Cisterciense* 4.26, in *The Great Beginning of Cîteaux: A Narrative of the Beginning of the Cistercian Order; The Exordium Magnum of Conrad of Eberbach*, trans. Benedicta Ward, Paul Savage, and E. Rozanne Elder, CF 72 (Collegeville, MN: Cistercian Publications, 2012), 369.

neither the day nor the hour when the bridegroom will arrive (Matt 25:13).[10] We watch because it is characteristic of lovers to watch for the return of the beloved. The foundress of the Focolare Movement, Chiara Lubich, has said: "Only love is watchful. This is a characteristic of love. When one loves a person, one watches and waits on him unceasingly. Every moment spent away from the loved one is lived with him in mind, is spent waiting. Christ asks for love, so He requires us to watch."[11]

How, concretely, might the night watch after Vigils be spent? If a two-hour interval is available, I might decide to spend at least one full hour in prayerful watching, recalling the words of Jesus to Peter in the Garden of Gethsemane, "Could you not stay awake for even an hour?" (Mark 14:37). My hour of watching with the Lord after Vigils may begin as soon as I have had breakfast, if I need that kind of stimulus to keep awake. Or I may begin my hour immediately after Vigils so as not to lose the momentum of prayerfulness built up during the chant. For the first quarter of the hour, I may linger in the church saying the rosary or other prayers. Then I withdraw to my cell for silent meditation. This is not my time for sacred reading but for watching and waiting in the prayer of silent listening. I may divide the time into two twenty-minute periods spent sitting or kneeling, with a five- or ten-minute interval between them, spent in another posture such as standing or walking slowly without interrupting my prayer. Changing position and stretching for a moment are natural ways of combating drowsiness without the aid of caffeine. In this way my hour of private watching passes fruitfully. Afterward I allow time for breakfast and washing up and may still have a short period left for sacred reading or other reading before Lauds. The creative use of time after the night Office will differ from individual to individual, but the general intention will be to watch for

---

[10] Jerome, commenting on this passage in Matthew 25, recalled the Jewish tradition that the Messiah would come at midnight and the Christian belief that Christ would return during the Paschal Vigil (J.-P. Migne, *Patrologia Latina* 26:192).

[11] Chiara Lubich, *Meditations* (New York: New City Press, 1974), 37.

the coming of the Lord, so that the hour of the master's coming will not catch us off guard like a thief (1 Thess 5:4; Rev 3:3; 16:15). Those who need additional sleep may take advantage of the afternoon siesta, as Benedict's Rule provides, but the time after Vigils traditionally has been reserved for watching in prayer.

Monks and nuns, besides being watchers, have other jobs that must be accomplished in the course of the day. Sometimes they have so many tasks that they feel tempted to rush out immediately after Vigils and begin their day's work. But the work of the day will be fruitful, and to the glory of God, only when we have renewed our personal relationship with the Lord in the silent hours of the early morning before the bustle and business of the day's activity have begun. By our watching and praying we consecrate to the Lord the first fruits of the day, and therefore all the work, the interactions, the unexpected events, the successes and failures of the entire day as well. Saint Paul enunciated the principle of the first fruits: "If the firstfruits are holy, so is the whole batch of dough; and if the root is holy, so too are the branches" (Rom 11:16).

Watching as Struggle

The night watch has lost none of its ascetical aspect through the centuries. Watching in prayer at night will often be felt as a time of struggle, a time of fighting drowsiness. Saint Isaac of Nineveh in the seventh century speaks for numerous monastic witnesses about the ordeal of night watches: "There is nothing so feared, even by Satan, as prayer which is offered during vigils. And even if it takes place with distraction, it does not return fruitless, unless that which is asked, should be what is not becoming. Therefore he engages himself in severe battle with them, in order to turn them away from this performance if possible, namely, those who are constantly at it."[12]

---

[12] Isaac the Syrian, *Mystical Treatises* vol. 2, no. 559, trans. A. J. Wensinck (Amsterdam: Koninklijke Akademie van Wetenschappen, 1923; repr. Wiesbaden, 1969), 374–75.

It is of the nature of vigils to be a test of the power of spirit against the power of flesh. In the garden of Gethsemane Jesus said to his drowsy apostles, "Watch and pray that you may not undergo the test. The spirit is willing but the flesh is weak" (Mark 14:38). Watching promotes and symbolizes the ascendancy of spirit over flesh in our life, and the final victory of life over death in our physical body, for the oblivion of sleep is the image of death. Watching strengthens and prepares us for the time of testing. The great adversary of night watching is not sleep so much as Satan, the ruler of the night. The person who watches and prays at night challenges Satan at the doorway of his domain, for the night belongs to him (see Luke 22:53; John 13:30; 1 Thess 5:4). The Desert Fathers and Mothers saw drowsiness as Satan's weapon to keep them from prayerful vigil.

Watching implies a clash of forces, a combat, a struggle. The agony of Jesus in the garden of Gethsemane was his struggle against the demonic power of darkness threatening to invade his heart and obliterate the light of his Father's will. Jesus, praying at night in Gethsemane, is the model for watchers. His spirit proved master of his flesh, so that when the soldiers came to arrest him they found him prepared, awake, at prayer, ready to submit to his Father's will. Jesus had asked his companions to watch and pray with him, but they all yielded to the weakness of the flesh and fell asleep; they were unprepared and fled in fright when the soldiers came. Because they did not watch with Jesus, they were not worthy to suffer, die, and rise with him.[13]

If we are looking for more contemporary models of night watching, we may think of many parents who watch during the night by a child's bedside when the child is ill or frightened. They lose their sleep, but it is out of love for their children. Love is always ready to watch and wait on the beloved one. The night nurse is on duty while her patient tries to sleep. Other examples might be a security guard in a building, watching for burglars, or a shepherd watching for predators that might attack the flock, or

[13] See Xavier Leon Dufour, ed., *Dictionary of Biblical Theology*, 2nd rev. ed. (New York: Seabury, 1973), 643–44.

a soldier on guard duty while his buddies sleep at night. These stay awake to guard against intruders. The monk stays awake with them to pray for them and pray for all those in need at that time—those in the final hour of their life, those who bear the cross of insomnia, those who devote themselves to sin at night.

Interior Wakefulness

The monastic practice of watching, begun in community at the office of Vigils and continued by the individual in his or her personal vigil, is ordered to an interior stage of wakeful vigilance, the awakened heart. In the Hesychastic tradition, this attitude of inner wakefulness is called *nepsis*, or sobriety, from Saint Paul's admonition to the Thessalonians, "We are not of the night or of the darkness. Therefore, let us not sleep as the rest do, but let us stay alert and sober" (1 Thess 5:6). A sober, wakeful heart is alert to the presence of the beloved and prepared for a visit. The bride in the Song of Songs exemplifies the watchful, responsive heart, listening for the approach of her lover: "I was sleeping, but my heart was awake. The sound of my lover knocking! 'Open to me, my sister, my friend, my dove, my perfect one!'" (Song 5:2). Our night watches and other monastic practices are aimed at awakening our heart and keeping it ready to welcome the Lord. "Behold, I stand at the door and knock. If anyone hears my voice and opens the door, I will enter his house and dine with him, and he with me" (Rev 3:20).

People may be physically awake, but they will not hear Jesus knocking at the door of their heart unless they are also spiritually awake and vigilant. Some are walking in their sleep spiritually, not yet awakened to the horizon of spiritual values. They are still gratifying their senses, accumulating more toys, trying to control their world. Likewise, a life with a "Do Not Disturb" sign permanently posted means that someone prefers dozing in a cozy, comfortable cocoon where everything is orderly and predictable. Clinging to possessions, as a toddler clings to a blanket, is another sign of a person's desire to lead a tranquilized, robotized existence.

Monastic life summons us to awake from the prevailing pursuit of worldly values. From the beginning of his Prologue, Saint Benedict calls for interior wakefulness: "Let us get up, then, at long last, for the Scriptures rouse us when they say: 'It is high time for us to arise from sleep'" (RB Prol.8; Rom 13:11). Monastic ascetical practices such as watching continually awaken us on a deep level of our being by disturbing the somnolence of our heart.

Awakening the heart is not a once-and-for-all event, for weak flesh is persistently inclined to take its rest. In this sense monastic life may be a continual sequence of falling asleep and waking up again. "I lie down and I fall asleep, [and] I will wake up, for the Lord sustains me," says the psalmist in a psalm that Saint Benedict chose as a preinvitatory for the office of Vigils the year around.[14] After every moment of awakening, there eventually comes a realization that what once seemed like daylight and wakefulness is a dark dormancy compared to the light about to dawn on us. Always there are new insights, new steps to be taken, and new doors to be opened in the work of spiritual transformation. The night watch that begins each day is a reminder of the need for continually renewed vigilance. Only when we finally awake in the kingdom of heaven will the process come to an end, for there the glory of God will generate an eternal day, "and there will be no night there" (Rev 21:25). Meanwhile we go on waking and sleeping, watching and waiting.

The monastic night watch is good practice in the art of waiting, as we patiently look for the coming of dawn. Monks and nuns wait in the dark night, longing for the light of dawn but unable to hasten its coming. No one can force the dawn or bring it about in any way. It dawns in its own good time on those who wait for it. The ability to wait is characteristic of those who have learned

---

[14] Ps 3:6 cited in RB 9.2. Abbot Damasus Winzen has drawn attention to the scriptural theme of sleeping followed by rising to a renewed existence. He refers to the sleep of Adam, Jacob, Elijah, David (in Ps 3), and Jesus in his death and resurrection. Rising from sleep becomes a symbol of Christ's resurrection and merges one's life more closely with his. See Damasus Winzen, *Pathways in Scripture* (Ann Arbor, MI: Word of Life, 1976), 180.

to slow down and live in the fullness of the present moment. Impatience with the rate of change and renewal in monastic life blocks a contemplative appreciation of the possibilities available right now. The night watch, repeated again and again, forms in us the habit of patient waiting and of calm abiding in the situation where God has placed us. We accelerate the process of spiritual transformation and maturation, of healing and integration, only at the risk of spoiling it.

Contemporary electronic media have accustomed many to expect results at digital speed, but the normal pattern of spiritual transformation is gradual and organic, two steps forward and one step backward. Rising early and waiting during the night helps teach me patience. By quietly watching and praying, I learn to live with the slow process of my own spiritual growth. I have no control over the future, and I do not know exactly what will happen. I am asked only to stay awake and be ready, because the light will surely come and will claim its victory over every form of darkness, despair, suffering, and death—yes, even over death, just as the victory of the Easter Christ took place "very early, when the sun had risen, on the first day of the week" (Mark 16:2). The monastic practice of watching finds its deepest meaning in the dynamic of the Paschal Mystery.

Conclusion

How long will it be before we fully share the victory of the Risen Christ in his kingdom? "A little while later and you will see me," said Jesus in his farewell discourse at the Last Supper (John 16:16). What are seventy, eighty, or ninety years compared to eternity? A little while. Saint Augustine says that when the little while is over "we shall feel how little it has been."[15]

Monastic life is about staying fully awake for this little while, awake in body and awake in heart. The night watch in our monasteries lasts but an hour or two; it is, nevertheless, rich in

---

[15] Augustine, *Tractates on the Gospel of John* 101.6, New Advent, http://www .newadvent.org/fathers/1701.htm.

symbolism and practical ascetical and spiritual value. The quality of our monastic search for God is mirrored in the way we watch for the coming of the Lord in our morning vigils. Monastic life has always meant a life of vigilance and a concern for the awakened heart.

Questions for Reflection

Isn't the monastic night watch outdated, because Saint Paul says that all Christians are children of the light and of the day, not of the night (1 Thess 5:5)?

Why is it that knowing the reasons for night Vigils, as well as having the right motives, does not make it easier to rise early every morning?

behold the true brotherhood which adversity cannot sever:

how good and how joyous to dwell together in unity!

COMMUNITY AND COMMUNICATION

The earliest monks, such as Saint Paul of Thebes and Saint Anthony the Great, lived alone. After some time, their location was discovered, and others joined them. Toward the end of his life, Saint Anthony was surrounded by disciples, each living as a hermit in a small hut. From there it was a short step to living under the same roof, and Saint Pachomius (292–346) is credited with taking that step into the cenobitic, that is, communal monastic life.

Saint Basil of Caesarea advocated cenobitism over eremitism or solitary life, because hermits had no nearby neighbors to provide opportunities for growth in virtue by serving others. Saint Benedict himself practiced the hermit life at Subiaco but wrote his Rule not for hermits but for cenobites, whom he calls "the strong kind" of monks (RB 1.13).[1] Communal monastic life today attracts people who are looking for support in practicing their

---

[1] *The Rule of Saint Benedict 1980*, ed. Timothy Fry (Collegeville, MN: Liturgical Press, 1981), 171.

religious ideals and who desire to live with people whom they can respect, trust, and love.

There is a correlation between the quality of our community life and the quality of our personal spiritual life.[2] The latter depends to some extent on the former. In the present chapter we shall discuss aspects of the common life that help bind dissimilar individuals into a unified community characterized by mutual loving service. From such a climate, our personal spiritual growth draws indispensable support.

In the Same Boat

When Thor Heyerdahl sailed from Africa to South America in a papyrus boat, it was not the ocean waves or the primitive vessel that worried him most, but the question of how the seven men aboard would get along with one another. They came from seven different countries and were of different ages, different religions, and different professional skills, and spoke different native languages, and they would be living shoulder to shoulder on a small boat for four months. In fact there were difficult moments, but all the men on board were genuinely committed to the expedition's goals, and so their voyage ended successfully, on a note of fellowship.[3]

A monastic community may be compared to Heyerdahl's papyrus boat. In the monastery we are all in the same boat, fellow travelers in an enclosed structure that we cannot freely leave. The voyage can be a joyful one or it can become a hell of loneliness, bickering, and suspicion that ends in shipwreck for all. The quality of our interpersonal relationships in the monastery is critical. If I am called to the cenobitic monastic life, I cannot seek God as if I were the only person on board. My way to holiness and personal wholeness lies through and with my fellow travelers.

---

[2] For a description of the interdependence of Christian community and Christian spirituality, see Jean Vanier, *Community and Growth: Our Pilgrimage Together* (New York: Paulist Press, 1979).

[3] Thor Heyerdahl, *The Ra Expeditions*, trans. Patricia Crampton (New York: Signet Books, 1972).

I will be faithful to my vocation and will find intimacy with the living God because of them, not in spite of them. Shipmates help one another reach their destination by being attentive to common needs and by affirming the contribution each one makes to the general effort.

We do not choose our shipmates. God chooses them. Monks and nuns come from various nationalities and backgrounds, have various levels of education, and feel differently about such important things as liturgy, work, sports, politics, food, cleanliness, punctuality, even theology and spirituality. We have different work ethics and different ideas about the way things should be done. We may belong to various generations or speak with a foreign accent. God in his wisdom has called us all to one place, to this monastic school of love, in order to learn to live and work together in peace and love. Our diversity is a blessing that enhances and strengthens the community.

Communication

In the chapter on silence, we saw that monks and nuns often prefer silence so as to be more available for constant communing with God. When we do speak, as we are free to do whenever charity or necessity prompts us, our words can be an articulation of that silence. Such words are life-giving and nurturing, because they are not born prematurely but after a full gestation in silence.

Saint Seraphim of Sarov, a Russian Orthodox monk, lived as a hermit for many years, devoting himself to silent, listening prayer. When people eventually discovered his hermitage and began coming to him in great numbers, they believed his simple, artless words to be a pure channel of the Spirit of God communicating life and truth. Seraphim's speech was a word out of silence, a word that was better than silence.

Saint Seraphim obviously had attained great holiness, and he exemplified a truth expressed in the Letter of James about control of the tongue, namely, that a person who is without fault in speech is perfect and is able to control his whole being (Jas 3:2). Monks and nuns are not strangers to faults in speech; we use our tongues to sing, "Praised be the Lord and Father," and then use them at times for uncharitable remarks to or about our brothers or sisters, "though they are made in the likeness of God" (Jas 3:9).

What sort of words should be avoided in the monastery? The list would be lengthy and should probably include idle chatter or adolescent chit-chat about every thought that flits through the mind: gossipy words, words that inflict pain and open or reopen wounds, filibustering words that do not let the other person break into my monologue, words heavy with cynicism and mockery, the words of off-color stories, words of backbiting or detraction.[4] Saint Benedict repeatedly cautions against words that spring from a spirit of chronic complaining, crabbing, criticizing, judging, murmuring (RB 34, 35, 40, 41, 53).

Caution is also advisable concerning words that may infringe on the privacy of others merely to satisfy curiosity. A busybody constantly monitors what others in the community are doing and why, when they go to town and for what, who visits them and what they talk about. When information about such matters is freely offered, it may be proper to discuss it and to share our own experience, but it is another matter to be nosy, put people on the spot, and oblige them to reveal personal information.

Ideally our speech will be respectful and cheerful. In this way we give one another the space in which to grow freely, and we become the persons that God in the richness of his creative love has destined us to be. Ideally, we are also sensitive to the effect our words and tone of voice have on others. The right word at the right time brightens the heart: "One has joy from an apt response; a word in season, how good it is!" (Prov 15:23). Joy comes also from an encouraging word, a special wish on namedays, birthdays, and anniversaries, or an appropriate compliment meant sincerely. Insincere compliments will be discerned as derision or condescension.

By our words we interact with others in a way that can build or weaken our fellowship. It is important to keep a line

[4] See Susan Annette Muto, *Approaching the Sacred* (Denville, NJ: Dimension Books, 1973), 135.

of communication open between ourselves and the rest of the community from the superior to the newest member, so that we are on speaking terms with everyone we live with, even though the degree of mutuality and sharing will not be the same with each. There are many different levels of communication.

The vitality in a community is partly a function of the communication among its members. Do we speak to each other at all? Does our conversation tend to stay on the safe, superficial level of small talk about the weather? Do our exchanges ever move toward a deeper level of sharing in faith, love, and trust, as we sincerely try to enter each other's world in order to understand and be understood from within? Community is built by communication on the deeper levels, in a climate of nonjudgmental openness, sincere truthfulness, and understanding cordiality. Such communication is mortar that cements the members together in a unity of fellowship and conviviality.

Community is promoted also by periodic occasions of celebration and recreation when the customary discipline in matters of food, drink, and conversation is relaxed in appropriate ways. Saint Anthony of the Desert once explained why he was "enjoying himself with the brethren" instead of meditating in his cell. Anthony compared the common life to a bow that might break if bent too much: "If we stretch the brethren beyond measure they will soon break."[5] Times of general relaxation permit exchanges on an informal level where new relational patterns can be knit in the community.

From Communication to Communion

In any community there are likely to be one or two people whom we find more congenial. We sense that we can share more deeply with them without fear of rejection or judgment. We will have more in common with these than with the others, although we owe fraternal charity toward all. Friendships spring up as we

---

[5] *The Sayings of the Desert Fathers: The Alphabetical Collection* 13, trans. Benedicta Ward, CS 59 (Kalamazoo, MI: Cistercian Publications, 1975), 3.

come to know one another better through conversing, working, and praying together. The twelfth-century Cistercian abbot Saint Aelred of Rievaulx (1110–1167) wrote a dialogue on friendship that is still studied today.[6] He had a wide circle of acquaintances but only a few close friends. Aelred made an effort to include Christ in these friendships, as he says to his friend Ivo, "Here we are then, you and I, and I hope a third, Christ, is in our midst."[7]

Some friendships may lead to a situation of codependence that might be called a mutual leaning-post society. Healthy monastic community permits meaningful relationships to flourish, but dependent relationships, where I persevere in monastic life only because a friend is continually there to prop me up, are not healthy. Genuine friendships between mature, independent individuals are important if community is to be more than a place where each resident permits the others to do as they please and no one gets in anyone else's way.

The psalmist comes close to describing community in the sense of a communion of mind and heart, exclaiming "How good and pleasant it is when brothers dwell together as one!" (Ps 133:1). Together in worship, together in common life, the members of such a community become integrated into a kind of oneness, into a deep spiritual and material sharing or communion. The Acts of the Apostles describes the embryonic Christian fellowship similarly: "The community of believers was of one heart and mind, and no one claimed that any of his possessions was his own, but they had everything in common" (Acts 4:32). In this description the spiritual unity of the community—whereby they were of one heart and mind—has a material manifestation in the sharing of property.

Saint Pachomius, founder of cenobitic monasticism, insisted on renunciation of private property by all who wished to live in the

[6] Aelred of Rievaulx, *Spiritual Friendship*, ed. Marsha L. Dutton, trans. Lawrence L. Braceland, CF 5 (Collegeville, MN: Cistercian Publications, 2010).

[7] Aelred, *Spiritual Friendship* 1.1, p. 55. For further reading about spiritual friendship, see Patricia Carroll, *Spirituality* (September–October 1996), http://www.catholicireland.net/aelred-of-rievaulx-on-spiritual-friendship. See also Basil Pennington, "Friendship," *Cistercian Studies Quarterly* 33, no. 4 (November 1998): 473–76.

koinonia, that is, the monastic community. Saint Benedict likewise envisioned a monastic community that was mostly self-contained and self-supporting. The members contribute according to their ability and receive according to their need. The lifestyle of monks and nuns points them beyond community, in the sense of a group of people living together in harmony with a shared economy, toward a true communion, a oneness of mind and heart, a sharing that reflects the life of the Holy Trinity.[8] Jesus once gave us a criterion by which to tell whether a Christian community is living in communion with him and with one another. He said, "This is how all will know that you are my disciples, if you have love for one another" (John 13:35). It is by the personal deepening of the human and spiritual life of each individual that the fullest possibilities of Christian community are realized.

Community of Love

In a monastery that is a school of love the monks or nuns hope to find a lifestyle, a tradition, and an environment that help them follow their God-given call. Each feels he or she has been invited by God to seek and love him above all and to find personal fulfillment in God rather than in marriage, career, or any other opportunities this world offers.

Outside the monastery it is often difficult to find a community of love. People act at cross purposes. To risk a generalization, the spirit of contemporary society is one of indifference, competition, and greed, not of love and mutual help. In contrast to this, and also generalizing, the monastery is a place where people have the same purpose, share the same basic vision of life, and "help one another grow in freedom to the fullness of their stature in Christ" (Eph 4:13).[9]

[8] See Baldwin of Forde, "Tractate 15: On the Cenobitic or Common Life," in *Selected Tractates*, 2 vols., trans. David N. Bell, CF 38 (Kalamazoo, MI: Cistercian Publications, 1986), 2:159–91.

[9] See William Lynch, *Images of Hope* (New York: Mentor Omega, 1965), 78.

When we talk about a community of love, it is critical to keep a realistic, nonsentimental, notion of love. If the expression of love I am waiting for boils down to seeing all the brothers or the sisters standing in a circle holding hands, my expectation is not realistic. Realistic love has to do with serving one another, helping someone who needs help, or doing something extra for the benefit of all, whether it is to tidy up a mess, haul out the trash, or clean a sink and toilet. Love is practical and willing to do its good works without being seen. "And your Father who sees in secret will repay you" (Matt 6:4).

Cenobites strive for a community of love that is mutual, not one-sided. Mutuality in love means that I cannot expect always to be the receiver of love, unless I for my part am first the giver of love. Saint Benedict singles out the father of the community as the special recipient of everyone's love: to their abbot they show "unfeigned and humble love" (RB 72.10). In response, the abbot is to avoid favoritism: "He is not to love one more than another" (RB 2.17). Building a community of love is the responsibility not of the abbot alone but also of every member of the community.

The Imperfect Community

My community does not have to be perfect in order for it to be a channel of salvation for me. No monastic community is perfect.[10] The community in which I actually live, with all its limitations, is the community where God, for hidden reasons, has placed me. I believe that here I can always, in every situation, find the link of love that connects me with God. Communal living can be enriching and fulfilling, but it can also be a penance, not only in the sense that I must patiently bear the infirmities of others as they do mine, but also in the sense that I must collaborate with them, in spite of their infirmities and my own, in the tedious process of resolving common problems and reaching common decisions.

---

[10] See the summary statement on the state of the Order by the Cistercian General Chapter of September 2008, *Minutes of Assisi 2008*, private circulation, Annex 6, 313.

The monastic community is home for us for a lifetime. We share life with one another and write together the history of our community. To the extent that I feel at home in my imperfect community, I can be myself, let my guard down, relax, drop the mask that I wear when I want to make an impression on outsiders. Within our community, each of us stands revealed before the others with all his or her strengths and weaknesses. Sometimes the common life is not pretty at all. That should never surprise us, because we are not always pretty ourselves. Recognition of our common human condition as wounded, but not mortally so, empowers us fully to share life's joys and sorrows with one another.

Accepting One Another

At times, in spite of good intentions, I fall short of my own ideal of openness and trust. In the concrete situation I find that others are annoying me. I fall back to a more primitive, prerational concern for my own security and satisfaction. Almost without realizing it, I manipulate my brothers or sisters for my own purpose by a variety of techniques—by flattery, anger, nagging, or a silent, martyred attitude. Such relationships are no longer based on the truth.

Truth is also lost from sight when I pin a label on someone and tell myself that he or she has not changed in twenty years and never will change. Labeling someone denies that person the space needed to change. Even should the other change, my preconceived image will not expand enough for me to recognize the change. The labels we pin on one another can read "dangerously progressive" or "hopelessly conservative" or "psychologically sick" or "senile and deaf." Before I can see change in another person, my inflexible view of him or her has to change. I have to see this person within the larger horizon of God's loving plan for each individual. Respect for truth makes me admit that my judgmental reaction to another's behavior may indicate a problem that is in me more than in the other. While the other is acting spontaneously and naturally, my reaction may be out of all natural proportion.

Living closely together in community challenges us to experience the variety of personalities as enriching and to feel comfortable with a diversity that sometimes obscures our underlying unity. Our unity is on the level of shared values; our diversity is on the more visible level of incarnating and living those values in a variety of ways. For the sake of unity I accept the validity of the other's monastic call and accept his or her way of responding to that call.

Acceptance does not mean accepting behavior that is harmful to the common good, but it does mean that I stop trying to change or refashion everybody so that they live as I would prefer them to live. I recognize that I cannot expect to change other people. God will change them in his own time, if he pleases, and when that time comes they will change voluntarily.

A deep, loving acceptance of others as they are means that I say yes to them at this time because they are part of God's will for me at this time. Acceptance does not necessarily mean praising them, nor does it mean blindness to their obvious flaws and woundedness. Acceptance means that I affirm this brother or sister whom God has called to this place for the sake of attaining the fullness of the stature of Christ. I uphold the human person who exists beyond outward appearance and behavior, beyond his or her past history of acting negatively toward me. Acceptance of the other person seems crucial for living harmoniously in community.

Forgiveness

In the real, as opposed to idealized, monastic community, conflicts arise. We are not like the two Desert Fathers who found they could not get into an argument: "Two old men had lived together for many years and had never fought with one another. The first said to the other, 'Let us also have a fight like other men do.' The other replied, 'I do not know how to fight.' The first said to him, 'Look, I will put a brick between us, and I will say it is mine, and you say, "No, it is mine," and so the fight will begin.' So they put a brick between them and the first said, 'This brick is mine,' and the other said, 'No, it is mine,' and the first responded, 'If it is yours, take it and go'—so they gave it up without being able to find an occasion for argument."[11]

In the civic community, conflicts are sometimes resolved by force, on the principle of "an eye for an eye." Sometimes they are resolved by litigation, which is a more sophisticated application of the same principle. In the monastic community, conflicts can be resolved and wounds healed by the gospel principle of compassionate forgiveness. Jesus expected his disciples to forgive as they have been forgiven, because all have their human failings.

Conflicts and injuries in monastic community, although unavoidable, are not desirable. One of the counsels of Saint John of the Cross needs to be interpreted carefully in this context. Saint John wrote, "You have not come to the monastery for any other reason than to be worked and tried in virtue, . . . you are like the stone which must be chiseled and fashioned before being used in the building. Thus you should understand that those who are in the monastery are craftsmen placed there by God to mortify you by working and chiseling at you."[12]

We know that we did not join the community simply to be worked over and treated like a stone for chiseling. Yet the Carmelite saint's counsel contains a kernel of spiritual wisdom. If the chisel-blows of painful words and deeds fall upon me, I can accept and bear them patiently for love of God, because they are experiences that help shape and season me in monastic life. The chiselers are not deliberately out to get me. They may not be aware of the abrasive effect of their deeds, or they may think they are doing me a favor by cutting me down to size. The advice of John of the Cross may help me to resist my instinctive reaction to pay them back in kind and give them a taste of their own medicine.

There may be occasions when I must confront someone out of genuine concern for his or her own good or for the good of others

---

[11] *The Wisdom of the Desert Fathers: Anonymous Series*, trans. Benedicta Ward (Oxford: Fairacres, 1975), no. 221, p. 60.

[12] John of the Cross, *Counsels to a Religious on How to Reach Perfection*, no. 3, trans. Kieran Kavanaugh and Otilio Rodríguez, *The Complete Works of St. John of the Cross* (Washington, DC: Institute of Carmelite Studies, 1973), 662–63.

in the community who may be involved. If the other accepts my correction in good spirits, our relationship will be strengthened and the air will be cleared. If I confront too quickly and clumsily, reacting from my own hurt feelings, the encounter is less likely to be productive. Monks and nuns sometimes prefer to go on enduring exasperating situations instead of risking an awkward confrontation. Skill and tact are needed to express legitimate anger or resentment in considerate ways that do not destroy a relationship but somehow communicate an underlying acceptance, forgiveness, and love of the other in spite of present differences.

A spirit of forgiving love is a key to living together. The First Letter of John states this principle: "We know that we have passed from death to life because we love our brothers" (1 John 3:14). In forgiving love we pass with Christ from death to life. Forgiving love opens our life to the power of the resurrection, enabling us to break through barriers into new possibilities, from mistrust to openness, from fear to love. The Paschal Mystery furnishes a model for interpersonal relationships in inevitable situations of friction, tension, and misunderstanding in the monastic community.

Often it is I who will have to take the initiative and forgive the other even before I am asked for pardon. Someone has to break the vicious circle of resentment and mistrust that can go from bad to worse as the days and months and years pass. Forgiving someone from my heart gives me an exhilarating sense of release and freedom, a paschal freedom. Also it gives the other an invitation to become the person he or she truly is deep within. Forgiveness up to "seventy times seven times" (Matt 18:22) is indispensable in common life.

I need to forgive for the sake of my own peace of mind, even if the other never asks to be forgiven. It is better to let go of the resentment and let it heal than to bear it for months or perhaps years like an open sore. Nursing a grudge does more harm to the one who refuses to forgive than it does to the one who caused the injury but may have forgotten it long ago. I can forgive in my heart even if I do not say it in so many words. By forgiving I become a healing, life-giving presence to others in my community.

Conclusion

Newcomers to monastic life define their relationship to the community over a period of time. At one moment the community may look like an ideal group of men or women, some of them exceptionally gifted and holy, who make the new member feel accepted, welcomed, and respected. At other moments the same community may be perceived as a hopeless collection of stubborn, narrow-minded, egotistical individuals who refuse to treat a newcomer as an equal. As the years go by, life in community will continue to be subject to this fluctuation; sometimes community life will be exhilarating, sometimes it will be a painful cross.

Perhaps such ambiguity is basically healthy. Any random grouping of people inclined to the monastic ideal is likely to be a mixed lot of admirable and deplorable elements, for such is the brokenness of our human condition. It would be unrealistic to expect to see only an angelic, or only a demonic, community. To see the community as simultaneously both, and to commit oneself to this community in all its human ambiguity, is the saving choice.

The astounding fact about monastic community is that in spite of our evident human brokenness and in spite of our evident personal diversity, we manage to live together for a lifetime in a peace and harmony that transcend all possible expectations. Ultimately it is the power of the holy and life-giving Spirit of God that makes us one, makes us a community. We remain a community because the bonding power of the Spirit of love is stronger than any divisive forces at work in our midst. Without the Holy Spirit we might end up destroying both the community and ourselves, as Saint Paul warns: "If you go on biting and devouring one another, beware that you are not consumed by one another" (Gal 5:15).

The monastic community, in which the members voluntarily live in close proximity under the lordship of Christ for a lifetime, has a transcendent faith dimension that cannot be found in apparently similar social groupings. There is an irreducible element of mystery in the very fact of monastic community life. The mystery of living joyfully in a community of love reflects something of the mystery of the Holy Trinity. Nourished daily by the eucharistic bread that is the body of Christ, the monastic community continues to bear witness to the living communion of the "children of light" (1 Thess 5:5) who constitute the Church and to the eternally shared life and light of the Holy Trinity.

Questions for Reflection

What do you see as the difference between conviviality, coexistence, communication, and communion?

What advice do you have for someone who feels a need for more communication but lives in a monastery with a strong tradition of silence?

i stand at the door and knock : if one should open

i will enter and sup, and we shall be intimate

THE MONASTIC CELL

Although monks and nuns live in a community, they are not always together in communal activities. Complete physical solitude is available in the cenobitic community behind the door of one's monastic cell. The word *cell* is used deliberately, instead of *private room* or simply *room*. Unfortunately, *cell* may suggest a prison, but it is the traditional monastic term going back to the earliest monks.[1] In the desert tradition, the monastic cell was called "the furnace of Babylon where the three children found the Son of God" or "the pillar of cloud where God spoke with Moses."[2]

In the solitude of the cell, the monk or nun encounters God. The monastic cell is the monastery in miniature, the monastery reduced to its basic components: solitude, silence, and the Spirit of God. In that sacred space that is both the physical cell and the

[1] See Jean Leclercq, "Pour une spiritualité de la cellule," *Collectanea Cisterciensia* 35, no. 1 (1969): 74.

[2] *The Wisdom of the Desert Fathers, Anonymous Series*, trans. Benedicta Ward (Oxford: Fairacres, 1975), no. 74, p. 24.

monk's or nun's heart, one can be occupied with God, listen to God. The enclosure of the physical cell leads the occupant to look within, to face himself or herself. That means facing the reality of who we are, including our history and our need for divine mercy.

Historical Development

For the Egyptian monks of the fourth century, the cell was their private oratory.[3] Just as they had a common oratory where they gathered for public celebration of the liturgy, so each monk had a private oratory for personal, solitary prayer; there the command of Jesus could be fulfilled: "When you pray, go to your inner room, close the door, and pray to your Father in secret" (Matt 6:6). In the secrecy of the cell it was possible to pray before God's eyes alone, not before the eyes of other people. In the gospel of Mark, Jesus sets an example by praying in solitude, outdoors, at night.

For two centuries the monastic cell, not the dormitory, was the general rule. The dormitory that characterized medieval monasteries was introduced at the beginning of the sixth century at the French abbey of Condat in the Jura Mountains.[4] When a fire burned down the monastic cells, a common dormitory was built instead, "as a necessary remedy to Gallican weakness."[5] The

[3] Some of these dwellings were uncovered in Egypt in 2005, intact since the fourth century. They were found several layers beneath the floor of the Church of the Apostles, St. Anthony's Monastery, in Zafarana, near the Red Sea. Michael Blackman, "Ever Since AD 270, the Need to Get Away From It All," http://www.nytimes.com/2005/09/28/international/africa/28monklife .html?_r=0.

[4] Historical information is drawn from John Baptist Hasbrouck, "The History of the Private Cell versus the Common Dormitory," *Monastic Exchange* 5, no. 1 (Spring 1973): 33–36.

[5] Hasbrouck, "History of the Private Cell," 36. In the same passage, Hasbrouck comments that historically, the introduction of the dormitory was a sudden change necessitated by intolerable abuses, not a move directly aimed at promoting the common life. He writes: "The abandonment of the cell for the common dorm signified the renouncement of the predominance of the contemplative orientation in favor of elementary good morals and the salvation of souls. The adoption of the dorm was not seen as something better in itself, but as a remedy for human weakness which had become too apparent."

specific weakness was not spelled out by the chronicler, but the dormitory obviously provided opportunities for surveillance that eliminated abuses of the private cell. Later in the sixth century Saint Benedict took it for granted that cenobitic monks would sleep in a common dormitory (RB 22.3), although elsewhere he says, "this porter will need a room near the entrance" (RB 66.2).[6]

In the eleventh and twelfth centuries the Carthusians and Camaldolese rediscovered the Egyptian tradition of the monastic cell. The mendicant orders of the thirteenth century adopted simple cells. In the fifteenth century Fra Angelico decorated the walls of several cells at the Dominican monastery of San Marco in Florence with masterpieces in fresco. The Benedictine congregations did not introduce the cell until the fifteenth and sixteenth centuries. The Cistercians initially adopted dormitories, but from the late thirteenth century they began partitioning the dormitories and even constructing private cells in spite of prohibitions from the general chapters of the fourteenth and fifteenth centuries. This development was influenced partly by the eremitical and mendicant orders and partly by sociological and cultural changes, such as the growing sense of the individual and of personal privacy.[7] In the seventeenth century Abbot de Rancé of La Trappe favored dormitory cubicles, but after the French Revolution, Augustin de Lestrange was content to partition the dormitory couches by heavy curtains.

The austerity of the common dormitory that formed part of the general severity of life adopted by the Trappist-Cistercian reformers resulted from their understanding of history and the principles of seventeenth- and eighteenth-century spirituality. In our own era, preferences have again swung back to the monastic

[6] *The Rule of Saint Benedict 1980*, ed. Timothy Fry (Collegeville, MN: Liturgical Press, 1982), 289.

[7] David N. Bell points also to the influence of new technology such as wall-fireplaces and improved chimneys, which permitted the heating of small spaces. See David N. Bell, "Chambers, Cells and Cubicles: The Cistercian General Chapter and the Development of the Private Room," in *Perspectives for an Architecture of Solitude: Essays on Cistercians, Art and Architecture in Honour of Peter Fergusson*, ed. Terryl N. Kinder (Turnhout: Brepolis Publishers, 2004), 188.

cell, and the majority of Benedict's disciples now rest, pray, or read in cells.

The Trappist-Cistercians authorized cells in 1967. Prior to that time, all slept in the dormitory in small cubicles open at the top, with a doorway hung with a curtain for a door. In returning to the primitive tradition of the monastic cell, the general chapter recognized a contemporary need for physical privacy and expressed its trust in personal responsibility that makes surveillance, and therefore the dormitory, unnecessary.

Spirituality of the Cell

Monks and nuns require formation in the beneficial and fruitful use of physical solitude for spiritual deepening. Solitude can also be a sterile, or even harmful, experience. There seems to be a natural human rhythm in the alternation between solitude and togetherness, between periods of openness and periods of closure. Thus I find support and companionship in the presence of my community, but at times in the course of the day I desire to withdraw to a private space where I can be in touch with my own individuality and can renew my personal dedication and love. That private space becomes a holy space for me, because it is there that I encounter God and also strengthen my ability to encounter God in other persons, situations, and events.

This solitary facing of myself and God is sometimes comforting, sometimes painful, but again and again I feel the need to alternate togetherness with aloneness. The unremitting closeness of living in community seems to cry for a balancing period and place of privacy. If I feel, even subconsciously, that someone is always breathing down my neck, then my defensive side is aroused and contemplative repose becomes harder to reach. Periodically putting a respectful distance between others and myself helps me later to interact more cordially with others in the community and also with God.[8]

---

[8] A Carmelite nun, accustomed to living in a private cell, wrote as follows in answer to a general questionnaire sent out by St. Joseph's Abbey, Spencer,

It is not that solitude has a higher value than community. Both solitude and the common life are monastic values, and they complement and balance one another. Both the capacity to sustain solitude and the capacity to relate easily with others are signs of maturity. In the solitude of the cell, I can come to a sense of who I really am. Yet it is by giving myself away in love of my neighbor that I also discover my deep self. In solitude I find the truth about the self I share with others.

A spirituality of the cell is based not only on the human need for privacy and solitude but also on the faith conviction that God is truly present in the monastic cell. The crucifix on the wall is a reminder that the cell is filled with the presence of Christ and is not merely an empty space where a person sits alone. Thomas à Kempis (1380–1471) wrote, "Shut yourself in, and call the well-loved presence of Jesus to your side; let him share your cell with you; nowhere else will you find such peace."[9] The divine presence transforms the monastic cell from a mere room into a kind of Eden where God and I can enjoy each other's company, with perhaps greater familiarity and spontaneity than is possible in the public oratory of the monastic church. In his Rule for Camaldolese hermit novices, Saint Romuald's first directive is, "Sit in the cell as in paradise."[10]

Massachusetts, in 1969 (unpublished): "Every person undergoes periods of special stress—whether physical, mental, emotional, or spiritual—and the opportunity to be alone to regain equilibrium and control can be a tremendous, and often truly necessary, help in enabling the individual to live his community life with less strain and therefore with greater fervor."

[9] Thomas à Kempis, *The Imitation of Christ*, trans. Ronald Knox and Michael Oakley (New York: Sheed and Ward, 1959), 45.

[10] *St. Romuald's Brief Rule for Hermit Novices*, trans. and commentary by Raphael Brown (Big Sur, CA: New Camaldoli, 1977), 4. In other respects, eremitical spirituality differs from that of cenobites, because the hermit's cell "is his entire universe," while cenobite monks find God not only in the cell but also in community and in the whole cenobium. On eremitical spirituality, see A Monk, *The Hermitage Within*, trans. Alan Neame (New York: Paulist Press, 1982), 140.

Dwelling in the Cell

In my monastic cell, in the presence of the Lord, I sit as Mary of Bethany sat at the feet of Jesus (Luke 10:39). Sitting is not so much a matter of posture as of attitude, the readiness to dwell, to remain, to abide steadfastly in the presence of the Lord. Initially the monastic cell might indeed seem too much like a prison cell, a place where I cannot bear to stay. I am not yet prepared to meet the cell's demand for interiority, for facing myself in all my poverty and for facing the Lord. I would prefer to go anywhere else, go for a walk, go and see what others are doing. It takes time to appreciate one's cell as a true sanctuary of the presence of God. It is by spending prayer time and *lectio divina* time in the cell that the sense of God's presence there intensifies.

If I cultivate the attitude of dwelling steadfastly in my cell, I will eventually be able to stay there with contentment. To quote the *Imitation of Christ* once more: "A cell lived in is a cell loved [*cella continuata dulcescit*]; little frequented, it will get on your nerves. Be a good tenant, a good caretaker to it when you first enter religion, and you will find it a cherished friend, a welcome consolation later on."[11]

The Desert Fathers and Mothers insisted on steadfastness in the cell: "Someone said to Abba Arsenius, 'My thoughts trouble me, saying, "You can neither fast nor work; at least go and visit the sick, for that is also charity."' But the old man, recognizing the suggestions of the demons, said to him, 'Go, eat, drink, sleep, do no work, only do not leave your cell.' For he knew that steadfastness in the cell keeps a monk in the right way."[12]

Running away is not the solution; I only carry with me the difficulties that surface in solitude. Steadfastness in the cell means that here I have chosen to take my stand until I learn to live with myself, with all my faults and failings, my emptiness and unfulfillment, as I wait in patience for the mercy of God to heal

[11] Thomas a Kempis, *Imitation of Christ*, 44.
[12] *The Sayings of the Desert Fathers: The Alphabetical Collection*, Arsenius no. 6, trans. Benedicta Ward, CS 59 (Kalamazoo, MI: Cistercian Publications, 1975), 9.

me and fill my heart and my cell with peace. The cell is the place where I hold my ground until I discover who I am and what I am called to do.

Thomas Merton wrote of discovering where we belong as monks and nuns: "Patiently putting up with the incomprehensible unfulfillment of the lonely, confined, silent, obscure life of the cell, we gradually find our place, the spot where we belong as monks: that is of course solitude, the cell itself. This implies a kind of mysterious awakening to the fact that where we actually are is where we belong, namely, in solitude, in the cell. Suddenly we see 'this is it.'"[13]

The spiritual masters of Egyptian monasticism promised their disciples that "your cell will teach you everything."[14] So it will, but I must not expect to learn everything in a single day. I will give my cell time, abiding there, waiting patiently until I can discern the subtle presence of God and hear his word in my heart. Abba Ammonas said, "A man may remain for a hundred years in his cell without learning how to live in the cell."[15] To live in the cell means to abide there faithfully and fruitfully. Time spent rearranging the furniture and reorganizing everything on the bookshelves does not exactly count. Steadfastness in the cell requires a docile, trusting attitude that gives the cell time to teach me everything and bring me fully to life. Dwelling in the cell and deepening my prayerful presence to God are fruitful not only for me but also for the life and salvation of others. By prayerful steadfastness in the cell, I can begin to heal in myself the wounds of the whole world that distress the Body of Christ.

Occupational Hazards

The monastic cell has at times been used in ways that are more harmful than helpful spiritually. We saw that abuses of the cell

---

[13] Thomas Merton, "The Cell," in *Contemplation in a World of Action* (Garden City, NY: Doubleday Image Book, 1973), 267.

[14] *Sayings of the Desert Fathers: Alphabetical*, Moses 6, p. 118.

[15] *Sayings of the Desert Fathers: Alphabetical*, Ammonas 96, p. 152.

led to the introduction of the dormitory in the sixth century. When there is a bed available, I may be attracted to studying or doing sacred reading in bed, or to taking frequent and prolonged naps. Or perhaps my cell becomes a clubhouse where those who belong to a small clique sometimes gather to socialize. My cell may serve as a private pantry where I keep food for a periodic snack. Poverty can be compromised if I give in to the temptation to decorate my cell excessively or with costly objects of art. Simplicity begins to be lost when my cell gets overfurnished and cluttered with souvenirs, posters, mobiles, and miscellaneous odds and ends that might, or might not, come in handy someday. It could be beneficial to spring-clean one's cell, discarding items of clothing and other things that have not been used for a year and that someone else might be able to use.

In some monastic traditions the cell is intended to be used as an office for intellectual and apostolic work. The necessary tools for this work may include a number of books and such equipment as a computer or sound system. The more such objects are needed for private use, the more important become the virtues of discernment and detachment. The virtue of charity would require that noisy equipment not be used when a neighbor is resting.

The cell may be misused as a refuge to which I can withdraw from the common life and barricade myself from others, from duties, from superiors, from the demands of community life. When others are looking for me, I can never be found. I turn my cell into a hideaway where I can pursue my own interests undisturbed. I have forgotten that a monk or nun is not a king or queen in a palace but one of the poor of Christ who no longer belongs totally to himself or herself but to God, to the Church, to the community, and to every child of God on earth.

At times the cell may also be the arena of combat with demonic forces that tempt the occupant to loneliness, boredom, erotic thoughts, or idle reminiscing. To expand on one example, loneliness is an obvious hazard for someone who spends time in physical solitude. It is quite possible to be solitary without being lonely. On the other hand, the presence of people is no assurance against loneliness. Loneliness can be felt at a community gathering.

Loneliness is a painful mood or feeling that comes when a person is separated from a loved one or from all company. Loneliness is a longing for that missing presence, a kind of sadness of heart, an anxious, distressful mood in which one is turned in on oneself. There are lonely hearts crying in the night even in monasteries.[16] If I choose to sit in my cell and indulge in self-pity, brooding over my unhappiness, I deliberately prolong and nurse my loneliness. With a little will power and creative imagination I might snap out of my mood and take a new interest in living.[17]

On the level of faith, I might reflect on lonely times as my sharing in the self-emptying of Christ who did always and only the things that pleased his Father, even when it meant drinking the cup of suffering and death. Loneliness teaches the lesson that my human heart will never find lasting fulfillment in anything or anyone except the infinite, unfaltering love of God.

Conclusion

The monastery is my home, but in my cell I have a home within a home, a place where I belong. In that place I can dwell securely and steadfastly, for this is the place where the Father wills me to be. In my own cell in my own monastery I am at home. Every time I enter and close the door of my cell, I experience a feeling of homecoming that is an inner event of peace and gladness. I know that the solitude of my cell conceals a loving, caring presence, the presence of one whose delight it is to dwell with the children of men (Prov 8:31). I do not have to leave the confines of my own cell in order to discover the Lord. The practice of steadfastness in the cell teaches me how to look beneath the surface of every situation in life, however dark, until I discover the light of God's will and God's love, without having to leave that place where God has willed to place me.

---

[16] For the moving account of a dream about monks struggling with loneliness, see Catherine Doherty, *Dear Father* (New York: Alba House, 1979), 24.

[17] Our context is loneliness, not depression. On clinical depression, see Evelyn Woodward, "The Depressed Religious," *Review for Religious* 39, no. 1 (January 1980): 43–66.

The monastic cell will be the scene of many struggles, defeats, and triumphs, many joys and many tears. The cell is like a womb from which I emerge again and again, reborn as a more mature, experienced self, ready once again to meet the challenges of the day. Perhaps my cell will be my infirmary room in times of lesser illnesses, or even the room where I will die, a tomb from which I will emerge to risen life. Steadfastness in the cell is the counterpart of stability in the monastery until death.

Questions for Reflection

In the monastery we do not belong to ourselves. Detachment from self and service of others are the path we have chosen. In this light, is the cell counterproductive to our monastic ideals?

What do you think is the major misuse of the monastic cell?

rooted in love, grounded in love, you will come to know

that love of christ which surpasses knowledge

STABILITY

Already in early monastic history, there was a breed of wanderers who called themselves monks but refused to settle down in any monastery. They preferred an itinerant style of life, seeking hospitality for three or four days at one monastery after another. Saint Benedict said they were "slaves to their own wills and gross appetites" (RB 1.11).[1] He called them "gyrovagues," literally, *wandering in circles*, and had no use for them.

Instead, Benedict insisted on stability—remaining in one's original monastic community. Stability is the practice of persevering, standing firm, staying where one has decided to live. Without explicitly saying it, stability implies permanence. There are hints in the Rule, however, that departures from monastic life were not infrequent. Benedict directed that monks who left the community might be readmitted up to three times in spite of their instability, if they seemed humble and repentant (RB 29.1-3).

---

[1] *The Rule of Saint Benedict 1980*, ed. Timothy Fry (Collegeville, MN: Liturgical Press, 1982), 171.

If there were problems with stability already in the sixth century, we should not be surprised that monks and nuns in our own highly mobile generation should sometimes find this practice difficult.

The Nomad Life

What value is there in promising to stay put in order to seek God in a particular community rather than in being free to go wherever the search might lead? The values of twenty-first century culture are contrary to the monastic practice of stability. It seems almost absurd to speak of staying in one place for a lifetime when we see people constantly on the go. They move to new houses, neighborhoods, cities, jobs, careers, even new marriage partners. We belong to an unstable society and have come to accept temporary arrangements as a way of life. Society is no longer surprised when, sooner or later, an old commitment is exchanged for a new one.

A percentage of the world's population has always been nomadic. In prehistoric times, when the human race was still in the hunting and food-gathering stage of development, everyone was a nomad. People had to follow the food supply, moving to warmer climates in the winter, constantly seeking new pasture and water for livestock. There are people who still live this way today: Bedouins in the deserts, Laplanders who follow the caribou, some Asiatic tribes, the Romany people, itinerant tinkers and traders. Such peoples create a culture of their own, but they are sometimes under pressure to stabilize in one place and assimilate into the surrounding culture.

In our time there are millions of people who are forced against their will to be nomads. They are refugees fleeing from a war zone, from an environmental disaster, or from oppressive conditions in their homelands. They end up in overcrowded camps and tent cities. They live in the modern diaspora, the great scattering of displaced people all over the globe. Our world is full of rootless, wandering, unstable people who have no place they can call their own.

Settling Down

Because we have different developmental goals to achieve at different times as we mature, it is normal to go through stages of life when we feel restless and other stages when we feel ready to settle down. The high rate of divorce and the number of annulments granted in the United States may be partly due to the fact that a lifetime commitment was made at an age when at least one of the partners was not emotionally ready or able to settle down permanently. Then, instead of accepting responsibility for nurturing a mature, stable relationship, the couple found it simpler to split up when serious difficulties arose.

When is one ready to settle down? It may be many years before one is exteriorly and interiorly ready to settle down permanently. It seems to me that in the normal course of development, stability is the appropriate achievement of the middle years of life, or, to attempt to pinpoint it more exactly, the mid-middle years approximately between forty-five and fifty-five. In some branches of Orthodox monasticism, there is a prudent custom of delaying the ceremony of bestowing the great habit that is the outward sign of permanent stability until one has lived the monastic life for twenty or twenty-five years. Depending on age of entry, this custom places permanent commitment near the time of the mid-middle years.

By the mid-middle years a person has usually found his or her niche in life and is prepared to stay there permanently. The phase of young adulthood, from the twenties up to about thirty-five, is past, with its search for career, for education, for profitable talents, for the single path or else a marriage partner. The next decade, from thirty-five to forty-five, encompasses early middle age. People are then at the height of their capabilities, managing projects, managing children, climbing the ladder in their professional field, influencing the scene around them in civic society or in the monastery.

This is also the time when people may run into unexpected obstacles that can throw them into a crisis, bringing up once again old questions about identity and vocation that they thought were resolved once and for all. Now these questions affect the meaning of life and can generate a cloud of darkness, self-doubt, loneliness, and uncertainty. Some people stay where they are and work through the crisis, coming out seasoned, reborn, more closely bonded with the important persons of their life, and endowed with genuine compassion, humility, and gratefulness. Others decide not to stay, but to make one last effort at a new beginning in a new situation, with the benefit of all their experience. As a result, during this phase of life there are dispensations from vows, laicizations, divorces, and annulments.

By the time people reach the mid-middle years (forty-five to fifty-five), they may be psychologically better prepared to settle down permanently. For several decades they have been constantly doing things, and now they become more appreciative of values connected with simply being: being themselves, being faithful, being here from now on, being fully present. As the years go on, it becomes more important to know that they belong somewhere, that they have a place where they are completely at home. As relationships grow more meaningful, it matters that they know where others are, and where they themselves are.

Seeking My Place

From the Jewish Hasidic tradition comes an instructive story about a man who was so scatterbrained he did not know where he was. The story is told by Rabbi Hanokh:

> There was once a man who was very stupid. When he got up in the morning it was so hard for him to find his clothes that at night he almost hesitated to go to bed for thinking of the trouble he would have on waking. One evening he finally made a great effort, took paper and pencil and as he undressed noted down exactly where he put everything he had on. The next morning, very well pleased with himself, he took the slip of paper in hand and read: "cap"—there it was, he set it on his head; "pants"—there they lay, he got into them; and so it went until he was fully dressed. "That's all very well, but now where am I myself?" he asked in great consternation. "Where in the

world am I?" He looked and looked, but it was a vain search; he could not find himself.[2]

The narrator, Rabbi Hanokh, added a comment of his own: "And that is how it is with us," suggesting that the man in the story was not so stupid after all, because he knew which question was most important. He had a problem with forgetfulness, but he was perfectly aware that the hat, pants, and other clothes he put on did not go to the heart of his whereabouts and identity in this world but only touched him exteriorly. There remained the fundamental question, "Where in the world am I?"

The question goes unanswered by many people who surround themselves with heaps of material possessions. In the midst of all their belongings, where do they themselves belong? The question is not necessarily resolved by shedding all one's possessions and joining a monastic community. In the Genesis story, Adam and Eve had nothing of their own except aprons of fig leaves, but they heard the Lord God call out this question as he walked through the garden in the cool of the day, "Where are you?" (Gen 2:9). They were hiding in the bushes, ashamed of their nakedness and disobedience. As long as they chose to hide and evade this question, they could not regain their relationship with the Lord.

Monastic stability gives people a place where eventually they can feel secure enough to stop hiding, come out of the bushes, be seen for the kind of people they are, and enter into honest, caring relationships with other persons and with God. For someone constantly on the move from place to place, it is less easy to enter deeply into such relationships, however much he or she may desire them. When we slow down, commit to staying, and let the good order of life flow around us, then we begin to see where we are and where our place is in the world. Renouncing our freedom to get up and leave at any time, we discover a freedom to explore the place where we are, to send down roots, to let ourselves grow, reach maturity, and produce fruit from deep within us.

[2] Martin Buber, *Tales of the Hasidim* (New York: Schocken Books, 1948), 2:314.

This kind of producing no longer aims at the glittering achievements and splendid successes that were the goals of young adulthood and early middle age but is the gentle unfolding of one's very being, like a blossom opening its petals in the sunlight. Monastic stability provides the soil and sun where one can become whatever one can be as a monk or nun.

Interior Stability

There is more to monastic stability than abiding bodily in a particular community. There is the further dimension of the interior feeling of contentment in the place where one has decided to settle permanently. Stability has two components, exterior and interior, and we may speak of stability of body and stability of mind or heart. Ideally exterior and interior stability go together. There are times, however, when exterior stability may be impossible because of special assignments or even political conditions, but a mature monk or nun continues to live in interior stability of heart.

An example of interior stability without exterior stability comes from the period of World War II when many European monks were drafted. They were required to leave their monastery for a tour of military duty. One of those mobilized was Fr. Gabriel Sortais, OCSO (1902–1963), of the Abbey of Bellefontaine in France, who eventually was elected Abbot General of the Cistercians of the Strict Observance. He became an army chaplain, constantly on the move. When he was free to return to Bellefontaine, he took up monastic life where he left off. Later, as Abbot General, he was again uprooted from his monastery and spent the remainder of his life visiting Cistercian monasteries in Europe, the Americas, Asia, and Africa. He managed to maintain stability of mind and heart, like a nomad with roots. His roots went deep into the mystery of Christ and the Virgin Mary. As the psalmist says, "He [was] like a tree planted near streams of water, that yields its fruit in due season; its leaves never wither" (Ps 1:3).

Usually, exterior stability serves interior stability. The first step is to stabilize the body in a particular community, a step that many take only after a long and difficult struggle. Even as we struggle to stabilize our body, we foresee the further task of stabilizing our mind and heart, the thoughts of our mind and the loves of our heart. These tasks may go on at the same time on different levels of the self. Any advance we make on one level, by quieting our wandering memory and imagination for example, is going to be helpful on other levels as well, because a human being is a composite of body and spirit, embodied spirit and inspirited body. All the monastic practices mutually promote this interweaving and reinforce one another.

The living core of exterior stability is stability of heart or at-homeness of heart. Without that living center, even if we spend our entire life in one place, our heart will wander, and we will not be truly steadfast, not at home, not at peace. Given that living center, perhaps it does not matter so much where we are physically and geographically, because the goal and value of monastic stability have been internalized and we carry them with us inseparably.

The Promise of Stability

The tradition of promising stability in the monastic community goes back beyond Saint Benedict (RB 58.17) to Saint Pachomius in the fourth century (Rule of Saint Pachomius 136, 175). Stability is to be distinguished from the practice of monastic enclosure.[3] The *Constitutions* of the Trappists define stability as a monk's response to God's call "to this place and to this group of brothers."[4] They speak of "enclosure" as regulating when outsiders may come into, or monks go out of, the monastery itself.[5] The promise of stability binds us immediately to a monastic community and, through the community, to the place where the community is

[3] See the distinction in RB 4.78: "The workshop where we are to toil faithfully at all these tasks is the enclosure of the monastery [*claustra monasterii*] and stability in the community [*stabilitas in congregatione*]."

[4] *Constitutions and Statutes of the Monks and Nuns of the Cistercian Order of the Strict Observance* (Rome, 1990), Constitution 9, p. 9.

[5] *Constitutions*, Constitution 9, pp. 22–23.

located. If the monastery has to move to a different place, as happens occasionally, then all the members move to the new place without detriment to their stability.

Saint Benedict's biographer tells the story of a hermit named Martin who wanted to guarantee his stability by fastening "an iron chain to his foot" and fixing the other end of it into a rock outside the cave where he lived. When Benedict heard of it, he sent word to Martin: "If you are a servant of God you ought to be bound by the chain which is Christ and not by a chain of iron."[6] Martin quickly complied.

Saint Benedict wanted monks and nuns to be bound by their own free choice, not chained so as to be physically unable to go anywhere else. Monks and nuns stay where they are for the sake of Christ, and not because of iron chains, bars, grilles, or high walls, and not even because of socio-psychological chains that might be stronger than iron and stone. Fear is the strongest chain, but Saint Benedict wanted monastic stability to depend on no chains but the love of Christ. On Saint Benedict's advice, the hermit Martin seems to have internalized the value of free, loving commitment to Christ, for when he cast aside his iron chain of fear, he proved that he could stay there without it. Love of Christ casts out fear from the heart (see 1 John 4:18).

Our promise to live permanently in one monastic community is not worth much unless it is a profoundly Christ-centered choice, something that draws us deeper into the mystery of Christ. This promise can be seen as the monastic way of saying yes to God's will for us in the place where we believe that God has placed us and with the task we believe God has laid on our shoulders. Thus, too, Jesus himself was steadfast and unswerving in his acceptance of the Father's plan for him, even when it meant being placed on the cross for the salvation of the world. Just as the cross in the end became Christ's place, monastic stability has to do with our own steadfast endurance of all the difficulties of life. Stability is

---

[6] Gregory the Great, *Dialogues*, trans. O. J. Zimmerman (New York: Fathers of the Church, 1959), 39:144.

our share in Christ's own steadfastness, his fidelity to his Father's will even to death on the cross, freely, out of love for the world.

Theological reflections can be crystal clear, but the twists and turns of life must also be acknowledged. Not infrequently monks and nuns become attracted to greener-looking grass on the other side of the enclosure. They may feel called to pursue their monastic vocation at a monastery where they hope to accomplish greater good with fewer obstacles. It is at such times of uncertainty that the promise of stability may strengthen their resolve and protect them from a rash move. Prayer, discernment, and consultation with superiors will help to reveal God's will. Circumstances can change, and Church law allows for a change of stability to another monastery.[7]

The Actual Community

The promise of monastic stability commits us to the community as it concretely is, with all its strengths and weaknesses, not to the community as it ideally should be. The actual community is the only community that exists, and by stability we throw in our lot with it for better and for worse. The English Benedictine cardinal, Basil Hume, has commented, "We give ourselves to God in a particular way of life, in a particular place, with particular companions. This is our way: in this Community, with this work, with these problems, with these shortcomings. The inner meaning of our vow of stability is that we embrace the life as we find it, knowing that this, and not any other, is our way to God."[8]

Thomas Merton likewise stressed the communal consequences of the promise of stability when he wrote,

> The real secret of monastic stability is, then, the total acceptance of God's plan by which the monk realizes himself to be inserted into the mystery of Christ through this particular family and no other. It is the definitive acceptance of his communion, in

---

[7] *Code of Canon Law* (Rome: Libreria Editrice Vaticana, 1983), Canon 684.3; *Constitutions and Statutes of the Cistercian Order*, Constitution 60, p. 51.
[8] Basil Hume, *Searching For God* (New York: Paulist Press, 1978), 78.

time and eternity, with these particular brothers chosen for him
by God to share in his sorrows and his joys, his difficulties and
his achievements, his problems and their solutions. It means
the glad realization of the fact that all who are thus called together will work out their salvation in common, will help one
another to find God more easily, and indeed that we have been
destined from all eternity to bring one another closer to Him
by our love, our patience, our forbearance and our efforts at
mutual understanding.[9]

If stability means sharing life, it means being with others both
in times of harmony and in times of struggle. In the life of Jesus,
there is an instance when he sought human support in a time of
struggle and found none. According to Matthew's description of
the agony in the garden, Jesus said to Peter, James, and John, "My
heart is nearly broken with sorrow. Remain here and stay awake
with me" (Matt 26:38). The word *remain* can also be translated as
abide, be united to, live in, dwell in, stay with. The qualities of the
monastic practice of exterior and interior stability are implicit in
Jesus' exhortation to "remain here and stay awake."

Exteriorly, stability is a promise to stay in this community
with Christ and with all the others and to stay awake in order to
support each other during the struggle. Interiorly, one's heart is
awakened to the needs and feelings of others, to the will and the
word of God in our midst. The contrary attitude would be to stay
in monastic life with increasing hardness of heart and dullness
of hearing until the sparkle goes out of our eyes and all we do is
hang around waiting for the evening news.

The Right Place

A story about Abba Sisoës (d. 429) in Egypt illustrates how
easily stability may be practiced if the place is right: "A brother
asked Abba Sisoës, 'Why did you leave Scetis, where you lived
with Abba Or and come to live here?' The old man said, 'At the

---

[9] Thomas Merton, *The Monastic Journey* (Kansas City, MO: Sheed, Andrews
& McMeel, 1977), 68.

time when Scetis became crowded, I heard that Anthony was dead and I got up and came here to the mountain. Finding the place peaceful I have settled here for a little while.' The brother said to him, 'How long have you been here?' The old man said to him, 'Seventy-two years.'"[10]

Abba Sisoës gave up his original stability at Scetis because of crowded conditions there and found greater peace and solitude on Anthony's Inner Mountain. The time sped by until seventy-two years seemed like "a little while" to him. Sisoës took root on the mountain and allowed himself time for patient growth and spiritual deepening like a seedling slowly reaching its maturity. Thus he became Abba Sisoës, a senior, an old master full of wisdom and grace, venerated as a saint especially in the Orthodox tradition.[11] This story does not tell us what Abba Sisoës did in that place. The chief point is that he was there a very long time, relishing his stability. He found the place peaceful when he went there initially, and he stayed long enough to let the peace of the place enter into the pores of his being until he radiated the peace he had absorbed. In his seventy-two years on the mountain, Abba Sisoës had time to come to terms with himself and with God.

If these realities can be experienced only by living as a hermit for seventy-two years, very few people will ever experience them. Instead, the lesson to be learned from the story of Abba Sisoës is that reaching one's full human and spiritual potential seems to be facilitated by some degree of stability in a place where one can be at ease, sort things out, and grow to spiritual maturity. For monks and nuns, the monastery is the right place for that kind of inner work. Within the monastery they may have a favorite place for deeper prayer, perhaps a corner in the church, or their private cell, or somewhere in the courtyard. Frequenting their own special place in the monastery, they may sense the underlying sacredness of any and every place.

---

[10] *The Sayings of the Desert Fathers: The Alphabetical Collection*, Sisoës no. 28, trans. Benedicta Ward, CS 59 (Kalamazoo, MI: Cistercian Publications, 1975), 283.

[11] Sisoës the Great, Orthodox Wiki: http//orthodoxwiki.org/Sisoes_the _Great.

The practice of stability helps us to look for the loving presence and power of God everywhere and in every situation. Wherever we are right now is the place where God's mysterious design has placed us and wants us to be. We have not been thrown haphazardly into this precise situation, nor did we drop here by chance, but we were placed here, deliberately and lovingly, for a reason that may become clear if we look for the signs of God's will in these concrete circumstances. Why are we here? What mission have we here for God, for others? The mystery of stability teaches us to experience every situation as the place where a divine loving will permits us to be at this moment of our life.

Being at Home

In the particular place where we have been placed, we can begin to feel at home. What does it mean to call a place our home? Is our home the physical environment of this monastery with its land, trees, fields, and mountains? Is our home the actual buildings in their particular layout and architecture? Or, within the buildings, is it our own private cell with its collection of personally meaningful, memorable objects and familiar furniture? Or is home not so much a geographical place but a person or a community of persons whom we know and love and by whom we are known and loved?

The final suggestion seems to come closest to the meaning of home, because even though we go back to visit a once-familiar place that we used to call home, it will no longer be home for us if we have no loved ones there. Home is associated with family, friends, relatives, loved ones, close companions. It is because of the relationships we have had with such people and because of the experiences we have shared that a place seems like home to us. Because of a community of persons or because of even one person, we feel welcome, secure, comfortable, trusted, accepted in this place. That familiar feeling is the feeling of at-homeness. We feel at home and feel we belong in a group where all share the same language, interests, values, and tradition. Monastic stability promotes at-homeness and makes it possible.

Not everyone in modern society knows this experience of at-homeness. People waiting in airports or confined to hospital are not at home. Refugees are not at home. Workers or students who spend years abroad do not always feel at home. Still another kind of homelessness has been described by existentialist philosophers like Martin Heidegger. The German term for this condition is *Unheimlichkeit*, the state-of-not-being-at-home in one's own existence or being. According to Heidegger, advanced technological civilization is no longer at home with the fundamental reality of being human, which is to be dependent on something greater than we are, namely, being itself, the Holy. Instead, we in technological cultures depend on things that are only the extension of our own powers, so that ultimately we depend on ourselves. Never going beyond our own potentialities and limitations, we have lost sight of our true center and source that is the Holy. Homelessness results when a civilization drifts away from the source on which it truly depends. Heidegger has said that human beings are meant to be "at home in the gathering together of all things."[12]

The practice of monastic stability fosters a gathering together that must take place within the individual before it begins to affect and humanize our civilization. Leading lives of recollection within the monastery, monks and nuns are engaged in a process of collecting or gathering together what has been dispersed or scattered within them, until they become unified, whole, together. The central core or source around which we strive to unify ourselves is, in monastic tradition, called *the heart*, that personal center of the self where the Holy makes its dwelling place if we are true to God's word (John 14:23). The Orthodox bishop and monk Theophan the Recluse said, "When we are in the heart, we are at home; when we are not in the heart, we are homeless."[13] Monastic stability leads us beyond the feeling of being at home

[12] See James L. Perotti, *Heidegger on the Divine* (Athens, OH: Ohio University Press, 1974), 96–98.

[13] Timothy Ware, ed., *The Art of Prayer: An Orthodox Anthology* (London: Faber & Faber, 1971), 192.

in our monastery to a stability of heart, stability in the love of God who makes a home in our heart.

Our monastic community is our home, but not in the same sense as our family of origin. Jesus has called us away from that family: "There is no one who has given up house or brothers or sisters or mother or father or children or lands for my sake and for the sake of the gospel who will not receive a hundred times more" (Mark 10:29-30). Like Abraham we have gone forth from our land, relatives, and father's house (Gen 12:1). We cannot expect the same kind of home life that we grew up in. Still, it helps to add little touches that contribute to a homey atmosphere in the monastery and dispel the feelings of an impersonal, uncaring institution. Informal touches might include things like cheerful colors, plants, flowers, carpeting, and furnishings that do not compromise monastic simplicity. An inviting, homelike environment depends even more on people with open, affirming, compassionate, joyful attitudes toward others. Newcomers are quick to sense the presence or absence of a welcoming spirit that puts them at ease and makes them feel at home in their new surroundings.

Homesick at Home

The monastery—the place where we practice monastic stability—is called three times in the Rule of Saint Benedict "the house of God" (RB 31, 53, 64). One principle that Benedict stressed was that "no one may be disquieted or upset in the house of God" (RB 31.19). We have a right to feel at peace in God's house because this is the community where we have been formed in monastic living and have come to taste and see how good the Lord is to all who live wholeheartedly in his house (Ps 34:8).

Yet the monastery is not our ultimate home. It would be unfortunate to forget about our true homeland (see Heb 11:13-16). Like Abraham and Sarah, we are "strangers and aliens on earth" (Heb 11:13), even though the whole cosmos can be called God's house. God is its builder and caretaker. We dwell in this house only temporarily, knowing that "our citizenship is in heaven" (Phil 3:28).

We can expect to feel a kind of homesickness in our present earthly situation, as if we were away from home. The feeling may come as a pang of incompleteness, of longing, of homelessness. The phrase "homesick at home" is from G. K. Chesterton's book *Orthodoxy*, in which he says, "I knew now why grass had always seemed to be as queer as the green beard of the giant and why I could feel homesick at home."[14] Chesterton had an intuition that the immediate situation, which might be as commonplace as the green grass growing on his front lawn, was actually part of a much larger reality where he knew he belonged and where all the separate parts could find meaning in a harmonious pattern.

There is a possibility that those who lead a well-ordered, regular life in a monastery may become encapsulated in their orderly little universe where security, piety, and mutual good will are taken for granted and no longer fully appreciated. In that case, it would be beneficial to experience a distinct sensation of not being at home that shakes us a little, gives us a twinge of anxiety, and knocks us out of the rut we are getting into. Similarly, in the life of prayer, the feeling of being dissatisfied, ill at ease, out of sorts, and not at home with our prayer may be an invitation to move toward a new stage or mode of relationship with God.

Stability and Environment

Visitors to a monastery are often moved by a sense of tranquility in the environment, even without attending any of the liturgies or meeting any of the monks or nuns. At one monastery, a young neighbor boy was an occasional visitor, riding over on his bicycle and spending a few minutes in the church. On one occasion the lad visited the reception room and told the monk on duty, "I feel good in your church."

A monastery does not acquire that discernible tranquility overnight but only after its walls have echoed for years with sung praise and silent longing and seeking, with the struggles and

---

[14]G. K. Chesterton, *Orthodoxy*, chap. 5, as quoted in James Schall, "Monastery and Home," *American Benedictine Review* 29, no. 4 (December 1978): 319.

victories of many monks or nuns. The relationship between the environment and those who live there in stability goes in both directions. The inhabitants influence the natural environment, and the natural environment has its subtle effect on the inhabitants. There is a symbiosis, that is, a mutually beneficial, cooperative, interdependent relationship between the environment and those who dwell there.

Stability will give us a sense of relatedness to our locale: to the land, the mountains or hills on the horizon, the rivers, lakes, or woods on the property, the wild animals and birds that are native to the area, the trees, flowers, and weeds that thrive there. Stability commits us to be good stewards of our locale and not abuse it. Locale extends to the buildings where we live and work. The natural world that surrounds us makes a unified totality of which we are component parts. We have kinship with the living realities around us that are intertwined with our life. The same molecules of nitrogen, oxygen, phosphorus, carbon, and hydrogen that flow through them are flowing through us, as will be even more evident when our bodies are buried and become part of the earth we now live from and live on.

We inevitably stamp our dwelling place with qualities of our own personality and temperament so that we can almost see ourselves as in a mirror in the environment we have shaped. If we enter the workshop or private cell of a friend, we notice how much the room resembles the owner. Perhaps we notice that there is a place for everything, and everything is neatly in its place, reflecting just the kind of person who lives there. Or perhaps we notice the opposite condition, a chaotic, jumbled, untidy holy mess, but how like the person who lives there! Over the years there has been a silent dialogue between place and person as they adjusted to one another. A harmonious relationship has been formed between them.

An example of the bonding and linkage of a person and his environment can be found in the life of Carl Gustav Jung. He had a home at Bollingen beside the upper lake of Zurich where he spent half a year at a time. He loved the place like another self and felt that it had entered crucially into his life's work. Jung himself built the central tower, learning from two Italian masons how to split and lay stone. Later, other rooms were attached, with arched openings, and a central courtyard of flagstone where Jung kept a neatly stacked woodpile. He chopped wood for his fireplace and stove, and pumped water from the well. Living close to the rhythms of nature, he confronted existential questions about the meaning and structure of human life. In his autobiography, Jung wrote,

> At Bollingen I am in the midst of my true life, I am most deeply myself. . . . At times I feel as if I am spread out over the land-scape and inside things, and am myself living in every tree, in the splashing of the waves, in the clouds and the animals that come and go, in the processions of the seasons. There is nothing in the Tower that has not grown into its own form over the decades, nothing with which I am not linked.[15]

Jung discovered what those who practice monastic stability discover, that it is deeply healing, humanizing, life-giving, and creative to dwell in one environment until we know its texture like another skin. We respond to the changes in our environment and adjust our relationships to the reality of nature, people, things, and events around us. Human life is affected for good or bad by the situation and surroundings that it gradually integrates into itself. Our environment grows on us and in us, and over the years we grow or fail to grow, humanly and spiritually, within it. There often seems to be a correspondence between exterior surroundings and human interiority, between the place outside and the place inside.

Constant exposure to a place as it is can help us acquire the ability to accept and appreciate reality itself as we find it in God's house. Over the years we can learn how to enjoy the common, simple things of life and to be happy in the present circumstances and the present tasks, because we are always drawing life from the larger mystery of life revealed in the familiar scene around us.

[15] C. G. Jung, *Memories, Dreams, and Reflections* (New York: Pantheon Books, 1963), 225, 214.

Conclusion

Reflection on the practice of monastic stability has shown how we can learn the art of accepting, appreciating, and valuing the place where we find ourselves and especially the other persons who share this place and will share it with us for a lifetime. For some people, stability will never be easy. According to the Bible, all creatures are unstable and transitory. Only God abides forever as the "rock of ages" (Isa 26:4). Monastic stability is designed to help us find our place and our peace in God.

We are in God as in a place, for "in him we live and move and have our being" (Acts 17:28). God is our place as men and women who practice monastic stability; in God we choose to establish ourselves and have stability. It takes a long time fully to realize that God is our place, that God is truly enough, that God alone is all we need and alone will bring us the peace and meaning we long for in life.

In our contemporary age of fast-moving, fragmented, driven, overstimulated, pleasure-and-profit seekers, the witness of a stable, peaceful monastic community is likely to attract visitors who find themselves renewed by pausing for a time to share the monastic tranquility and prayerfulness. When they leave, they may carry with them a resolution to live a more God-centered life themselves. In this way, the monastery gradually has a stabilizing influence on the surrounding society, like leaven in the dough that permeates and transforms everything that comes into contact with it.

Questions for Reflection

In terms of stability, what is the difference between inmates serving life sentences in the penitentiary and monks or nuns with solemn vows in a monastery?

Do you foresee that a permanent commitment to one small corner of the world will lead to forgetting the needs and concerns of the larger world?

what we shall be has not yet been revealed, but when it is,

we shall be like him, for we shall see him as he really is

FROM DEATH TO LIFE

Being a monk or a nun is not a short-term venture but a way of spending one's whole life. A person joins a monastery and pronounces vows in order to stay there for the rest of his or her life and ultimately to die and be buried there. Once an abbot was showing a prospective postulant around the monastery, and he said to the young man: "Should you enter, we will take care of you from then on; if you get sick, there's the infirmary; if you die, there's the cemetery." The candidate's startled reaction showed that he had not been thinking that far ahead.

In our time, many people are willing to talk about death, even their own eventual death, and to consider what will happen to their body after death. Death is not a taboo subject, as was sex in the Victorian era. Dealing with death is a big business. Morticians know how to make a corpse almost more beautiful than the person was in life. Besides the traditional cemetery, there are choices for a green burial site, also called "natural burial."[1] For people who

---

[1] See for example Cool Spring Natural Cemetery in Berryville, VA, https://www.virginiatrappists.org/cemetery; and also Honey Creek

choose cremation, there are options for a columbarium.[2] For those who prefer a casket, noble but less expensive models are available.[3] Books on death and near-death experiences have been best sellers: *The Tibetan Book of the Dead*, Raymond Moody's *Life after Life*, Elizabeth Kübler-Ross's *Death: The Final Stage of Growth*, Anita Moorjani's *Dying to Be Me*. There are death-and-dying seminars, popular lectures on the ethics and theology of death, university courses on thanatology. Some people are not afraid to arrange their own funerals before they die. Many companies offer aerial burial services and will, for a fee, disperse the ashes of cremated persons from an airplane. One person paid a large fee for the privilege of being dispersed over Africa, because it was a place he had always wanted to visit. Some of these developments may be silly and not all are Church approved, but at least people are squarely facing the issue. They realize that sooner or later they will die; they prepare themselves for it; they learn to cope with their fear of it.

Facing Death

Fascinated by alleged medieval rituals surrounding death, some sectors of the public are curious about our monastic funeral customs. As a matter of fact, however, we monks are not people morbidly preoccupied with death, who dig our own graves a shovelful each day and drink our beverage from a skull-cup! Nor do the monks and nuns of today deliberately hasten death by practicing extreme austerities. In the past, it is true, there was a different mentality in some monasteries. Saint Bernard apparently ruined his stomach by overzealous fasting in the first

---

Woodlands in Conyers, Georgia, http://www.trappist.net/abbey-trades /conservation-burial-ground/.

[2] See Columbarium at Mepkin Abbey, Moncks Corner, South Carolina, http://mepkinabbey.org/wordpress/wp-content/uploads/2011/09 /columbarium-brochure.pdf, and also Place of Peace Columbarium in Bristow, Virginia, http://osbva.org/html/News.html/.

[3] For example, Trappist caskets handmade at New Melleray in Peosta, Iowa, http://www.trappistcaskets.com, and also Saint Joseph Woodworks in Saint Benedict, Louisiana, http://saintjosephabbey.com/woodworks.php/.

five or six years of his monastic life and after that had difficulty keeping food down; he allegedly required a special receptacle at his place in choir in case of emergencies.[4] While still valuing and practicing asceticism, today we try to take prudent care of our health, though without going to the opposite extreme of body-sculpting and multiple health food fads. We get medical attention as we need it, and when sickness or accidental injuries happen, we try to accept them as part of the human condition. Lying on a sickbed provides an opportunity to review one's life and put one's goals and priorities in order. If the illness is serious, we can request the sacrament of the anointing of the sick.

The fact that monks and nuns long for the eternal life of heaven does not mean that we despise our temporal life here on earth. Temporal life is something good, a valuable and noble gift that God has given us, not something to be rejected. Thus we can pray with the psalmist, "I plead, O my God, do not take me in the midst of my days" (Ps 102:25).

Anyone who has lived the monastic life for some length of time has probably seen at least one death in the abbey. Although it is not always the case today, according to the classic scenario, the dying monk or nun is in the infirmary. When death seems imminent, the infirmarian notifies the superior, and the bell is rung to assemble the community for recitation of the prayers for the dying. After death the body is washed and laid out, then carried to the church, where a continual vigil is kept beside it, and the psalms are recited in a low voice until the funeral Mass begins. The funeral usually takes place within a couple of days unless there is a reason for embalming the body and delaying the funeral. In the monastic cemetery beside the church, the body is respectfully lowered into the grave, back to the mother earth from which it was taken, "the common ground which bears us all" (Wis 7:3; see Gen 2:7). It is customary to remember the deceased with special prayers and Masses.

---

[4] On the difficulty of diagnosing exactly Bernard's health problems, see Jean Leclercq, *Bernard of Clairvaux and the Cistercian Spirit*, trans. Claire Lavoie, CS 13 (Kalamazoo, MI: Cistercian Publications, 1976), 16–17.

The death of one of our monastic brothers or sisters is an occasion for us to reflect in a peaceful, simple way about our own approaching death. Thomas Merton has written, "A monk who does not think of death, and does not have it before his eyes, and does not see it as it is, and see his own life objectively in the light of death, cannot be a true monk. His penance will be unbalanced and his intentions will not be pure. His contemplation will be largely an illusion. His relations with his brothers and his whole life and outlook especially in his work will be natural and vain."[5]

It is the fact of facing death that gives monastic life its depth of realism. For the monk or nun death is always on the horizon, and life is a continual, accelerating movement toward death and beyond death. For those who love God, death is a door that closes on one form of life and opens into another, more abundant and untroubled, form of life. "I came so that they might have life," promises Jesus, "and have it more abundantly" (John 10:10).

The death that we confront is not death in general, but our own personal death, our own eventual ceasing to be here. The personal recognition of death goes so totally against the grain that some have doubted the possibility of its true recognition.[6] We shrink from admitting that this self of which we have grown so fond and which we have so carefully been bringing to full maturity and integration for sixty, seventy, or eighty years will one day be snuffed out like a candle. We instinctively resist the truth that this whole confused and fascinating, complicated and delightful process of living will one day end for us while it goes on for everyone else.

---

[5] Thomas Merton, *Monastic Orientation* series 5, no. 23 (mimeographed edition, Gethsemani Abbey, 1953–1954), 77.

[6] Sigmund Freud held, "It is impossible to imagine our own death [because we can always perceive] that we are in fact still present as spectators. Hence the psycho-analytic school could venture on the assertion that at bottom no one believes in his own death, or, to put the same thing in another way, that in the unconscious every one of us is convinced of his own immortality." From "Thoughts for the Times on War and Death," Standard Edition, vol. 14, p. 289, cited by A. W. Richard Sipe, "*Memento Mori: Memento Vivere* in the Rule of St Benedict," *American Benedictine Review* 24, no. 1 (March 1977): 97.

So there are people who refuse to think about their own death; the subject is too depressing. Or they try to delay or outwit death, like the chess-playing knight of Ingmar Bergman's *The Seventh Seal*. Or they subconsciously attempt to escape death by constructing a symbol of immortality for themselves.[7] They try to write or paint or create immortal works to be respected and appreciated long after they themselves are gone. They may try to mold someone into a perfect replica of themselves, so that the father will live on in the spiritual or natural son who is his living image, or the mother in her daughter. People try in these ways to cheat or deny death, because deep down they feel that death is terribly unfair, they were born so that they might live, live fully and forever. The open acknowledgment that death is not right or fair is a healthy step. In the Bible, the skeptic Qoheleth observed long ago that death is on the horizon for every living thing: "The lot of mortals and the lot of beasts is the same lot: the one dies as well as the other" (Eccl 3:19). Death, however, is not the ultimate horizon. For those who have Christian faith and hope, the ultimate horizon is resurrection and life.

Letting Go

The renunciations of monastic life are practice for death. Death separates us from everything and everyone, forces us to let go of persons, possessions, vitality, self-image—everything. We prepare for this final loss by loving acceptance of the "hardships and difficulties that will lead [us] to God," the deprivations of monastic life, and the sacrifice of our own will or comfort (RB 58.8).[8] David Steindl-Rast has compared the vows to an anticipated death: "Death strips man of all external possessions; the monk anticipates this stripping by being content with the bare necessities of life. Death deprives man of his biological vitality; the monk freely imposes upon himself fasting and sexual absti-

---

[7] See Ernest Becker, *The Denial of Death* (New York: Macmillan, 1975), 268ff.
[8] *The Rule of Saint Benedict 1980*, ed. Timothy Fry (Collegeville, MN: Liturgical Press, 1982), 267.

nence. Death means the end of man's pretended independence; the monk cuts clear through that pretense by submitting himself in discipline to a guru, a master, a spiritual guide."[9]

Of course, a person may anticipate the stripping process of death without entering a monastery. Life itself seems to provide enough opportunities for letting go for anyone willing to make use of them. A married person may quietly accept throughout the course of his or her life that stripping away of possessions, bodily vitality, and independence that those in a monastery surrender all at once by means of vows, until, as Steindl-Rast says, "in their last hour they are both alike, both totally stripped, both perfectly open for the encounter with the absolutely unknown."[10]

Death takes us whether we want to give ourselves at that moment or not. In the monastery we practice denying ourselves so as to give ourselves—to others, to God, to the demands and duties of everyday life. Jesus reminded us that whoever would save his or her life will lose it (Luke 9:24). The one who will save his or her life is, paradoxically, the one who has the courage to stop grasping and holding on to life and instead risks letting go of everything. Clutching and hanging on is merely grasping at straws. Letting go feels like dying but actually releases us into the flowing stream of deeper life and meaning. Letting go is a moment of self-sacrifice, a moment of submission to a greater power. The monastic practice of offering up little sacrifices of self-denial throughout the day trains us to flow with life, to give ourselves in countless situations so that we know how to do it at the moment of death.

Accepting death is not quite so hard for someone who has had ample practice in letting his or her unrealistic, inappropriate, inopportune desires and ideas die without clinging to them and hanging on to them for dear life. Every time we submit out of love to the death of a selfish desire, we surrender ourselves a little more totally to the Lord who holds us in his infinite love and

[9] David Steindl-Rast, "Why a Man Becomes a Monk" (privately printed manuscript without date or pagination).
[10] Steindl-Rast, "Why a Man."

care. At the moment of physical death, this ingrained habit will prompt us to surrender our life, as Jesus did, to the inscrutable mystery that conceals God the Father's loving care: "Father, into your hands I commend my spirit" (Luke 23:46).

Beyond Death

Death is not merely the sloughing off of the body while the soul flies away like a bird. Death is the moment when I, who experience myself as a body-soul totality, come to an end, definitively. Death is what happens beyond all the "Life after Life" experiences remembered by people who have not gone so far that they could never come back. What lies beyond death?

We do not know, except by Christian faith, what lies beyond this life. In death we lose everything without knowing for sure that there is anything to follow. Our faith, however, assures us that there is much more ahead. There is the realm of the supernatural, the realm of the triune God, a God who is like a loving father or mother. Ultimate reality is not extinction, not the quenching of a candle flame, but God. Theologian Hans Küng has written, "The believer knows only that what awaits him is not nothing, but his Father."[11]

As Christian believers, we also know that the death and exaltation of Christ is the model and pattern of our own personal history as Christians and as monks or nuns. Christ opened a passageway through death to the life of risen glory, and we follow him through the breach. We expect, beyond our death, the surprise of resurrection, the free gift of God's glory. The sacrament Christ left as a memorial of his passion and death is the center of monastic life, our daily plunging into the life-giving Paschal Mystery. We encounter that same mystery of dying and rising in other ways in the course of our monastic life. Saint Benedict saw this rhythm of dying and rising as the underlying dynamic of monastic life: "Faithfully observing his teaching in the monastery until death, we shall through patience share in the sufferings

[11] Hans Küng, *On Being a Christian*, trans. E. Quinn (Garden City, NY: Doubleday, 1976), 359.

of Christ that we may deserve also to share in his kingdom" (RB Prol. 50). Faithful perseverance in the monastery implies repeated immersion into Christ's Passover, his going beyond death into eternal life and glory. When Saint Benedict advised us in the forty-seventh instrument of good works, "Day by day remind yourself that you are going to die" (RB 4:47), he was not being morbid but saying, in other words, "Keep in mind that breakthrough into life and glory that you are continually accomplishing!"

What will it be like in that life beyond death? It will be the same I myself who live, but in a new body-soul totality. Saint Paul assures us, "What you sow is not the body that is to be but a bare kernel of wheat, perhaps, or of some other kind; but God gives it a body as he chooses, and to each of the seeds its own body" (1 Cor 15:37-38). We will live in a new continuum of time called eternal life, the now that stands forever and does not pass away. Eternal life is perfect life, blessed life, life with God in an ever-deepening experience of communion, face-to-face vision, and love that never comes to an end. Saint Gregory of Nyssa (335–395) said, "This truly is the vision of God: never to be satisfied in the desire to see him; but one must always, by looking at what he can see, rekindle his desire to see more."[12] We will never find it boring to explore and admire, together with the angels and all the others present there, the inexhaustible depths of the mystery of the triune God.

Now and at the Hour of Our Death

In that perfect life beyond death, we shall rejoice to share the intra-trinitarian movement of knowing and loving, being known and loved. The wonderful thing is that this experience can begin essentially already on earth through the mystical dying and rising that occur in the stages of the life of prayer. The mystical traditions of various world religions contain a common teaching on the necessity of experiencing a death of self if one is to be united

[12] Gregory of Nyssa, *The Life of Moses* 2.239; see also 2.306, trans. A. Malherbe and E. Ferguson (New York: Paulist Press, 1978), 116.

with the divine (John 12:25, 2 Cor 4:10). That death may be phys-ical death at the end of earthly life, or it may be a mystical death of renunciation and surrender that takes place during earthly life but has certain parallels with physical death.[13]

Every significant loss, such as the loss of one's youthful strength and health, the loss of family members or friends, the loss of cherished dreams and plans, the loss of ego-ambitions and self-image, is a little death. Each time we gracefully go through a little death-and-resurrection event in our life, we mature more into the person we are meant to be and are more prepared for our physical dying and rising at the end of this life.

The mystical death of total surrender issues in a feeling of ex-hilarating freedom, a rebirth on a new plane of life. Total surren-der, however, is frightening and arouses anxiety and resistance. The anxious feeling we have is a sign that we are being invited to move beyond our present state of complacent existence into a new and closer relationship with the hidden God. We experience this invitation as a kind of death. Those who have assisted dying people have described several stages of response to the proxim-ity of death, although not everyone experiences all the stages.[14] Elizabeth Kübler-Ross proposed five stages in the 1970s, and her description has withstood the test of time. This typical pattern is one that occurs again and again in the course of life, not only at its end. We may have gone through some or all of these stages in the process of initially accepting our monastic vocation, or at various times during deep prayer, or on the occasion of a serious accident or sickness.

A brief summary of the five stages will help to identify them. The stages are successive responses to the approach of death on the part of someone who believes in God. The first stage is an instinctive reaction of denial, born of fear and resistance: "No,

---

[13] In a series of three articles, Linda Maxwell has shown that a death of self is involved both in mysticism and in physical death. See "Mystical Con-sciousness and Dying," *Contemplative Review* (Summer, Fall, Winter 1977).

[14] See Elizabeth Kübler-Ross, *Death: The Final Stage of Growth* (Englewood Cliffs, NJ: Prentice Hall, 1975).

not me, not now, I don't believe it, this can't be happening!" Denial leads to the second stage, resentment, a feeling of being wronged, even an anger toward God: "Why me, O God, why me? What have I ever done to deserve this?" Third comes some form of bargaining with God in which the dying person promises anything to escape death: "If you give me a little more time, I will devote myself entirely to serving you; I will be a changed person, you'll see." When all these efforts prove of no avail, the dying person is obliged to recognize his or her fate. The result may be the fourth stage, namely, a mood of depression and self-pity: "Yes, I am dying, and I am scared; there are so many things I wanted to do in life, so many opportunities missed, so many sins and failings." If there is movement past the stage of fear and depression, a person may finally accept the inevitable and, in so doing, come to a deep feeling of peace: "Okay. I am ready. You have called me, O God, and I am coming." This final stage, not always attained, is the stage of surrender.

Surrender to death and to God does not mean that we despise life as we have known it. It is when life is being snatched away that we truly appreciate it. Before that, we took life for granted, we played with the meaning of life. It is in the process of dying that we touch life most centrally. If we are told we have terminal cancer, we no longer take life for granted. We realize that we are no longer in control of our future; we cannot call the shots any more. We become aware of our utter dependence, poverty, insignificance, fragility. If we have been accustomed to a life of letting go, giving ourselves in service, surrendering and emptying ourselves, then these feelings will not be new. We will be ready to accept death from God's mercy as we have accepted life. Until the hour of death comes, however, we certainly will live fully and gratefully every moment of life that God allots us.

An eighteen-year-old youth first confronted the possibility of his own death when he heard a sermon on the fragility of human life and soon afterward felt an unexplained pain in his left leg. His imagination suggested that he was marked for an early death. The leg pain disappeared after some weeks, but was replaced by a breathing difficulty, the sensation of choking. He began to see

life in a different light, not as a totally unlimited project for the
future but as a free gift from God, given day by day. He learned
the importance of living in the present moment rather than looking far ahead to a future day that might never be given to him.
By choosing to live and to appreciate the present moment, he
was preparing himself to accept the moment of his actual death.

Theologian Yves Congar has expressed the opinion that "in the
Christian view of things . . . there are ultimately two important
and absolutely supreme moments: the present moment and the
moment of our death."[15] In the Hail Mary, we ask Mary to pray
for us at these two critical moments (now and at the hour of our
death), which someday will converge and be identical. These
two moments matter "because they are the meeting points with
God." If our hearts are awakened to God's voice in the present
moment, we have already begun our entry into eternal life and
glory, a journey that will be completed at the hour of our death.
A Christian, and especially a monk or nun, need not be anxious
about the morrow (Matt 6:34). Our concern is to live the present
moment of grace in accordance with the will of God. Some of
the saints, when asked what they would do if their death were
revealed to them as imminent, replied that they would carry on
with the work they were doing at the time. As a person lives, so
will that person die. One's last moment, Congar observes, will
be like all the others except for its finality, "and for the fact that
it seals, consummates and sums up all the others."

Conclusion

Again and again throughout this study of monastic practices,
we have encountered the life-producing movement of the Paschal
Mystery, but nowhere more centrally than in these reflections on
death. The best preparation we can make for death is to live the

---

[15] Yves Congar, "Nunc et in hora mortis nostrae: The Christian Understanding of Death," in *Faith and Spiritual Life*, trans. A. Masson and L. C.
Sheppard (New York: Herder and Herder, 1968), 204–14. The quotations in
this paragraph are from pp. 207–9.

reality of the Paschal Mystery as fully and as deeply as possible in union with Christ, because Christ will relive that mystery in us at the hour of our death. If we are following the spirituality of the Paschal Mystery, we can expect to die and rise again many times in the course of our monastic life, in our daily tasks and duties, in unexpected events and circumstances, in times of disappointments and utter failure, and in our life of interior prayer. We can expect to have to let go and give up again and again, discovering a new richness of life each time. We will draw nourishment for our piety from the Eucharist and the sacraments through which we participate mysteriously in Christ's own going over from death to life. Gradually we will learn not to be surprised at our own or others' frailty and finiteness. We will remind ourselves that the Father loves all his children and especially those who most need to depend on him because of their own infirmity. We learn to trust more and more this Father whose essence is love and into whose hands we shall one day, freely and gladly, hand over our life (Luke 23:46). On that day our final act of dying will be inserted irrevocably into the saving death and resurrection of Christ our Lord.

As an example of a monk's life of fidelity to monastic practices, and his death in the context of the Paschal Mystery, we can refer to a brother who died at the Abbey of Gethsemani in Kentucky at the age of seventy after twenty-eight years of monastic life:

> He loved his work and he loved choir, and during his intervals, he sat in church with his Psalter. His was an enviable balance. Each morning he was hidden in the cheese lockers washing the mold from every wheel of cheese we ate or sold. This he did for practically all his monastic life. And, in the afternoon, he came to be identified with the cows and calves, and to know each of them in a personal way . . . . This was Ferdinand until that Sunday in early January when he sent for Fr. Timothy to come to his room and help him. Cancer had galloped through him, fired up his old ulcer, and sped him away so fast that he really had little time to adjust to his infirmary schedule. Yet, despite his occasional bewilderment, he seemed to be hastening to keep an engagement which his Psalter always kept before his

mind's eye. For the Lord proposed that he should join Him in His own *transitus*. Br. Ferdinand died on Wednesday evening of Holy Week. We watched with him and the Lord through Holy Thursday. He was buried at the time usually reserved for the Psalter on Good Friday morning. And the Gospel of the Good Thief was read.[16]

Living the monastic life is sometimes difficult, but it is beautiful to have lived it, to be able to look back, at the moment of death, and realize we have done the best we could with the help of God's grace, and then to look forward to keeping an engagement with the Risen Christ. Such people die in peace, as much as it is possible to die in peace. The true monks and nuns are those who persevere to that final moment. We celebrate their funerals with alleluia and blazing paschal candle, because our brother or sister has joined the Lord in the final passing over to life and glory. Having shared by patience in the sufferings of Christ, they now find themselves being welcomed to share in Christ's kingdom forever. Their monastic practices culminate in an unimaginable ecstasy of endless joy.

Questions for Reflection

Would you prefer to be buried in a coffin or without one? Why?

What would you do if you were informed that you had only one hour left before a fatal heart attack?

---

[16] Br. Francis, "Going Home to God," *Regional Mailbag*, a publication of the USA region of the Order of the Cistercians of the Strict Observance, no. 87 (April 21, 1978).